Ultralight Aviation Series/No. 2

Ultralight Airmanship

Jack Lambie
Revised Edition

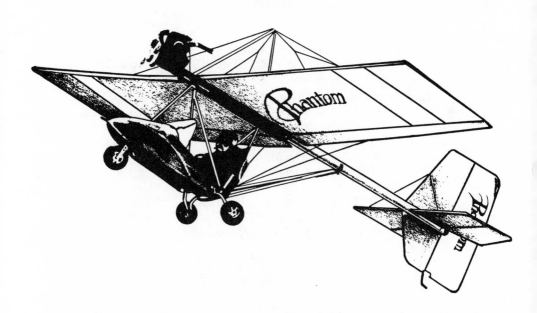

How To Master The Air In An Ultralight

Ultralight Airmanship
How To Master The Air In An Ultralight
Jack Lambie

Copyright © 1982 & 2001 by Michael A. Markowski

Published by:
AViation Publishers
One Oakglade Circle
Hummelstown, PA 17036
email: avipub@aol.com

Books by the Author
COMPOSITE CONSTRUCTION FOR HOMEBUILT AIRCRAFT

Library of Congress Cataloging in Publication Data

Lambie, Jack H., 1935-2000
Ultralight Airmanship –
How To Master The Air In An Ultralight
(Ultralight Aviation Series, No.2)

1.   Airplanes – Piloting.I. Title
TL710.L356   629.132.523   81-71888
ISBN 0-938716-02-6 (Paperback)

On the Cover

The Phantom features conventional independent three-axis aerodynamic controls, including full span ailerons. It is powered by a Rotax 447 single carb engine of 40 hp. It can also be flown with the optional 503 Rotax. Designed to FAR 103, it offers maximum allowable performance. An optional folding wing, as well as an enclosed version, are now available. Courtesy of Phantom Aircraft Company, 6154 West G' Avenue, Kalamazoo, Michigan, 49009. Phone:(616)375-0505;email:phantom@complink.net;website:www.phantomair craft.com; Pat Schultheis, President

Dedication

This book is dedicated to Otto Lillienthal and to the group of creative and enthusiastic people who gathered on a hill at Corona del Mar, California, on May 23, 1971 to celebrate Otto's 120th birthday. The 14 hang gliders present at this first meet in history were the crude forerunners of the Ultralight Movement.

To them, that event and the happy memories we shared in striking the match that lit the fire of the simple and basic flying machine.

Acknowledgement

Thanks to Captain Edmund Burke for his consultation and advice on FAA rules, proof reading; Irv Culver, on the direction of circling in thermals; Joe Greblo, Mike Meier, and Taras Kiceniuck, Sr. on turning theory; Dr. Paul MacCready on angle of attack in wind gradients; Jess Fich for comments and copy service; Mark Lambie for traffic patterns; Bill Lambie for drawing materials and advice; Mike Markowski for deadline insistance; and, word processing anc tea by Fran Gionet.

WARNING — A WORD OF CAUTION

Flight, in and of itself, is not necessarily dangerous, however it is most unforgiving of errors, sloppiness and misjudgment on the part of both the designer and pilot. Whenever a man flys, he accepts the risk that he may be injured or even killed. It is each individual's decision to either accept or reject this risk in light of its potential hazards, challenges and rewards. Flying can be and is done safely every day of the year by paying strict attention to the details.

This book is not intended as a do-it-yourself guide, but merely as a source of information to be used as a reference. If there is anything you don't understand, don't hesitate to ask your flight instructor. It is further recommended that you obtain a student pilot solo license and ground school before you attempt flight on your own. Ultralights are real airplanes, not toys, and they must be treated with respect.

About the Author

Jack Lambie is on the frontier of so many diverse activities the usual question is, "What are you doing next?" A lifelong love of the air and things that fly and move through it has been the focus and concentrated energy of Jack Lambie's life.

In 1978 he received the Soaring Society of America's Exceptional Achievement Award as a member of the design team of the Gossamer Condor, which performed the first successful sustained, maneuverable, man-powered flight. He has worked with Dr. Paul MacCready and Dr. Peter Lissaman previously as chief consultant, designer and vehicle tester on a National Science Foundation project to develop devices that reduce air drag on large trucks.

A student of bird flight, Jack raised many soaring birds. He has built models and full size sailplanes and gliders, as well as replicas of the 1901 and 1903 Wright Gliders and Flyers. With over 6,000 hours in 67 kinds of aircraft, holder of commercial and instructor ratings, he has also gained international soarings highest badge—the Diamond C (USA #20). A winner in many soaring contests, he was also the co-pilot on the flight that holds the current U.S. two-place goal record for gliders.

One of the founders of hang gliding, his "Hang Loose" design was built by the hundreds in 1970-71. As pilot, technical advisor, plane designer and builder, he has worked on many films and ads such as the PBS special "Orville and Wilbur," and the NBC "Winds of Kitty Hawk."

Jack and his wife Karen are the first couple to have ridden around the world on a tandem bicycle. Their 515-day journey covered 30 countries. He built one of the earliest streamlined bikes and co-organized the first of what are now annual human-powered speed contests. Almost 60 mph has been reached with the streamlined, advanced bicycle-like machines.

Aided by the National Geographic Society, he completed an 8,000 mile flight during 1980, in a motorglider to Paraguay, South America, exploring the Andes and searching for the great Condors.

Jack has degrees from the University of Illinois, USC, and UCLA and has been an educator for 15 years in primary, elementary, high school, adult and university graduate science programs. He was the first Director of Education for the California Museum of Science and Industry at Los Angeles, where he developed many innovative programs.

He has had 10 dozen articles published in various magazines, and a book published on gliding. Jack prowls the skies in his Fournier motorglider. He lives in Orange, California, where he divides his time between lecturing, writing books and working on fascinating projects.

Foreword

For decades, the age of "flight-for-everyone" was heralded to be here. In fact, ever since the Wright Brothers created the first powered airplane in 1903, it has been predicted that everyone would soon be flying as commonly as riding bicycles.

It just never did seem to happen, even after the hundreds of World War I Jenny trainers were sold cheaply and Barnstormers spread the thrill of flight to thousands. The "Golden Age of Aviation" from 1925-1939 was hailed by some as leading to a new era of flight. World War II ended that hope for awhile. Then, thousands of returning service pilots were expected to continue flying and carry us all into the air. Light plane builders went out of business or cut their production drastically, when "it" just didn't happen. The Experimental Aircraft Association became popular with homebuilders, which kept a large group of enthusiasts flying, but still no "flying-for-everyone."

Hang gliders became a rapidly expanding sport in the early seventies and, in the last few years, ultralight airplanes have grown out of these lightweight gliders when engines were added. It seems that the "Golden Age of Ultralights" and perhaps "flying-for-everyone" has finally arrived!

Flying is one of the most inspiring of activities because it so expands our understanding of the world. We can become as a molecule of air in lightly loaded ultralight flying machines, sensitive to every movement of the air. In driving a car, we must follow the road as it has been constructed. In the air we are free to make all of our own roads across hills, lakes and streams, according to our best judgment or whimsy. Especially in an ultralight is the pilot captain of his ship, primarily because he is able to land many more places than a regular airplane.

A person who goes into ultralight flying with no formal power plane instruction will find it difficult to find published information about the specific problems of ultralights. The standard "book" on flying airplanes discusses radio procedures for navigation, communications, air traffic control, instrument flight techniques, and high altitude cruise control. The flyers of ultralights are concerned with winds, weather on a micro scale, low and slow cross countries with simple navigation, and using small fields. As the ultralight winds its way across the countryside, its' pilot is more secure knowing how to gain altitude in natural lift and how to keep out of conflict with regular airplanes while using uncontrolled airports.

There's no question that ultralights can fly happily and safely in little wind and over their home field. But, this limits the joyful exploration and rich adventure that is traditional in flying.

The ultralight pilot who is in command of every situation and understands the possibility of dangerous conditions is, by far, a safer flyer. The confidence in being able to navigate by pure pilotage is a warmly satisfying achievement that takes us back to the pioneer days when flying was fun.

This book is for the ultralight pilot who already knows the basics of flying well. It is assumed the pilot will have several months experience and understands the fundamentals of flying the plane. Specific suggestions about control movements and flight techniques differ far more between ultralights than regular airplanes. A brief section on methods of turning smoothly in the main types is included, but to repeat each method during the discussions in the rest of the book would be redundant. I usually describe maneuvers applying the standard aileron, rudder, and elevator system because it covers the widest range of ultralights. Besides which, many flyers have some experience with regular airplane controls, making it easier to understand. Those flying ultralights with different controls, such as weight shift, tip rudders, spoilers, etc., should visualize particular maneuvers according to their own control system.

It has often been said that, "climbing in Dust Devils, running along the edge of a squall line, flying in the wind or making cross country flights should never even be considered ultralight flight activity." Some may say flying in waves or storms is dangerous, but what may be completely unsafe, or even foolhardy for one pilot may be quite safe for another. I believe a flat statement like that is nonsense without taking into consideration the type of ultralight, the pilot's knowledge, experience, and actual conditions. Real foolhardiness is shown by the attitude, "those things shouldn't be done in ultralights, therefore, I shall ignore even the possibility of learning about such advanced flying."

A real feeling of confidence and flying safety comes only through a sensible awareness of your own limitations and judgment. The more this is expanded, the more flying experiences are available within the realm of your own safety. Knowing these limits is better than blindly trying to fly "safely" and doing nothing that is even remotely challenging. In the air, conditions can change quickly. A turbulence, unexpected and unseen, can upset the most careful pilot, but not one who has learned to extend his knowledge and skills of flight. The experiences and knowledge of 35 years of flying gliders, hang gliders, very light planes and ultralights has been gleaned to give the most practical help to those who fly on the low speed frontier. Welcome aboard as we explore the various realms of ultralight airmanship.

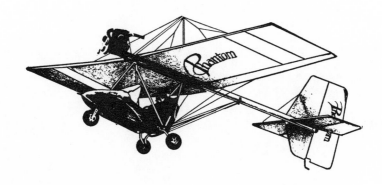

Contents

Introduction

There are 1700 ultralight airplanes sold every month and the activity is proving to be the equal of motorcycling and off road vehicle sports. With the sudden expansion of this newest form of flying-for-everyone, the hardware has gotten slightly ahead of the software. Until now no single book, with all the lore of the air in a readable style specifically aimed at the ultralight flyer, has been available.

The invisible ocean of air in which we are bottom dwellers is one of the last frontiers in the expansion of our experiences and understanding of the world. The tremendous energy available to the ultralight pilot is often unknown to them. Instead of boring through the air, flying only in the morning or evenings for fear of "bumps," the ultralight flyer can learn to use the power of the atmosphere to increase his performance and safety as well. Many new pilots learn by word of mouth, heresay, and lots of practice. A clear and definitive guide to the atmosphere and how to fly in a way to use its power and decrease its dangers is a must for any serious ultralight pilot.

This book covers the whole mysteriously wonderful world of the air, from the thermodynamics of gases, large weather systems and circulations to the details of micrometerology around valley passes, behind rows of trees and buildings. Above all, Ultralight Airmanship is a practical book because it tells exactly what to do and how the pilot is to fly his aircraft to make use of, counter and/or fly safely in all these conditions with specific advice and flight descriptions by experienced aviators.

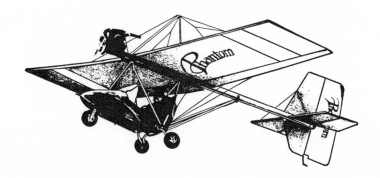

Parachutes· Safety First

A wonderful safety feature of ultralight flying is the availability of lightweight parachutes that lower you and the plane down together. In regular airplanes, pilots don't wear parachutes because it's difficult to get out of the aircraft, and they often have several passengers. I have witnessed three fatal accidents where the flyers had parachutes yet were unable to use them. One was a collision, in another the wing broke off, and the other one went out of control. In all these accidents the pilots would still be enjoying our company if a quick opening chute had been attached to the plane.

A parachute should be as much a part of an ultralight as the propeller. There are several being made that mount to your ultralight with propeller proof lines and a quick opening device. Even at low altitude, if you have a collision, control failure or wing break, you can pop the chute and land safely without leaving your seat!

Ultralight gliders have universally accepted the parachute, and powered ultralights should follow their lead. Parachutes are available from:

Ballistic Recovery Systems, Inc.
2277 W. County Rd. C
St. Paul, MN 55113

Eipper Aircraft, Inc.
26531 Ynez Rd.
Rancho, CA 92390

Handbury Products, Inc.
44 East Hayes Street
Bunning, CA 92220

Midwest Parachute
22799 Heslip Drive
Novi, Michigan 48050

Mitchell Aircraft Corporation
1900 S. Newcomb
Porterville, California 93257

Pioneer International Aircraft, Inc.
Pioneer Industrial Park
Manchester, CT 06040

Chapter One~
The Basics of
Turning Flight

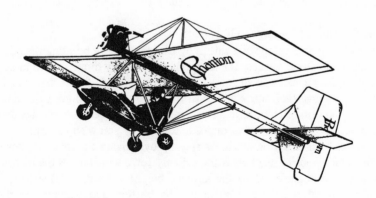

The Basics of Turning Flight

Flyers reading this book are already able to turn, but the major emphasis for most of the maneuvers needed for soaring and flying in winds is on precision turns. Therefore, this chapter will discuss some of the intricacies of going around in the air.

How an Ultralight Changes Direction

The only way an airplane can turn is by banking, not by pointing the nose. This is often misunderstood because the things that we usually move around in i.e., cars, make flat turns. The tires on a car are touching the ground. As the driver steers, the front wheels change their angle and push on the ground, producing the side force that enables the vehicle to turn. In an airplane, the force needed to change direction must come from deflecting the air opposite to the way you wish to turn.

All heavier-than-air flying machines stay up by moving a mass of air downward —an equal and opposite reaction is the primary force which holds the plane in the air. This force is transferred to the airplane by the secondary effect of pressure differences around the wing—positive on the bottom and negative on the top.

To turn, the wing must be tilted so that its deflection of the air will force the plane into a new direction. Simply pointing the nose the way you want to go will not make the plane turn, unless it slides through the air sideways for a distance. This causes the plane to bank, which only then will deflect the air sideways.

The rate of turn is determined by the mass of air being deflected, as compared to the weight of the airplane. A very light airplane with a large wing can make a quick turn with very little bank because it doesn't need the reaction of much air to

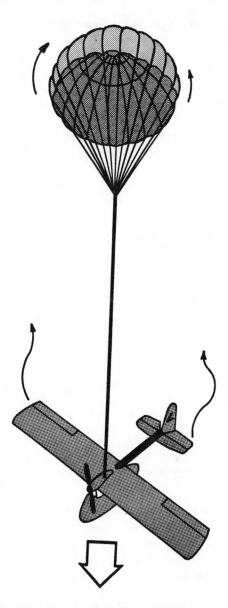

Fig. 1-1. All ultralights should have a parachute. If it's attached to the airframe, the pilot stays seated while deploying the chute.

change direction. Some sailplanes can turn in small circles using such a small bank angle that it seems as if they are skidding around. A jet fighter must bank almost vertically to turn, yet still takes thousands of feet to get around a circle because it's so heavy and the wing is so small.

Just as a car driven around a sharp corner at high speed requires a lot of side force, with tires scrubbing, so a plane in a quick turn needs more side force. It gets this force by tilting its wing very steeply and pitching up more strongly.

Doubling the speed of an airplane will increase the lift four times. That means the sharper you want to turn, the more the plane must be banked and the faster it must go. The nose must be pitched up enough to have the wing meet the air strongly enough to deflect it and force the turn.

Controls and Stability

At ultralight flying speeds, ailerons have only approximately one-fourth the air pressure acting on them compared to a conventional light plane. That, combined with the "apparent mass" effect, makes for a slow roll and adverse yaw problems.

Apparent mass does not bother heavy airplanes because they fly so much faster and there's plenty of control force. To understand apparent mass, think of moving a two pound paddle back and forth edgeways in the water. Because little water would be moved, it is easy to swing. Flat against the water it's very difficult because a greater mass of water must be moved. So it is with an ultralight wing. It is not just a few pounds of aluminum tubing and dacron that must be tilted to start a turn, but the entire mass of several hundred pounds of fellow traveling air. This is why weight shift is popular and works very well with hang gliders and ultralights.

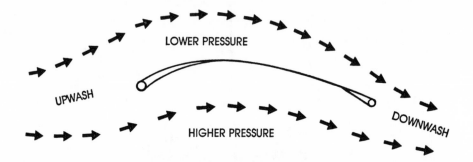

Fig. 1-2. A wing is like a turning vane — in deflecting air downward, it generates the reaction called lift.

For both low and high speed control both weight shift and aerodynamic controls are used in many ultralights. Lines are connected to the pilot's seat, so that when the pilot moves back and forth or side to side to change the balance, he also moves a rudder or elevator. Weight shift for pitch control is fast and easy, as there is less apparent mass to be changed in that axis. As mentioned before, banking is more difficult.

One problem with weight shift is when the plane drops, either in a dive or from turbulence, making the pilot momentarily weightless. (You can't shift the CG if you don't weigh anything!) Some of the early hang gliders with motors had a high thrust line. When stalled, the nose dropped. At pitchover, the flyer was lifted out of the harness. At the moment of nosing down with power on, the high thrust line would result in an increasing dive from which the pilot could not recover.

As ultralights become more sophisticated, many are featuring three axis aerodynamic controls. The machines operate like any other airplane except their roll rate is slow and there may be lots of adverse yaw. For roll, some designs use spoilers on the top of the wing. These flip up to destroy lift, causing it to drop and drag back. This neatly eliminates the adverse yaw of a wing with a down aileron. Some ultralights however, have no roll controls at all. Just as we found on the

Gossamer Condor human-powered project, aerodynamic damping was so great, and pressures so low, there was no use putting ailerons or spoilers on the wing. Ultralights without wing controls use a rudder to slide the plane sideways and rely on the banking induced by the dihedral to turn.

There are two parts to a turn. The roll and the pitch up. In a conventional rudder, aileron, and elevator controlled airplane, the sequence for a continuous

Fig. 1-3. A bank redirects the lift, causing the plane to turn.

circle is this; the stick and rudder are moved in the same direction at about the same time to start the bank. The rudder is used only because the wing with the downward angled aileron has more drag (adverse yaw) than the one with the aileron up. The rudder corrects for adverse yaw — that's it's function.

If the rudder were not used to counteract the drag of the upgoing wing, the plane would bank alright, but slide through the air sideways with the nose pointing opposite to the way you wish to go. Sliding sideways creates a lot of drag. The lower wing would be angled more directly into the wind which would tend to roll the plane back level again, since it has more lift even with its aileron up. That's why the rudder must be pushed, not to turn the plane but to keep the higher wing with the down aileron from being pulled backwards by the extra drag due to its increased lift (This is known as induced drag).

The wing must be at a positive angle to the oncoming relative wind in order to deflect air, so the stick is pulled back enough to push the plane around the turn. If the stick is not held back, the plane will spiral down.

In weight shift ultralights, a roll is accomplished by moving your weight to one side in order to start a bank. A combination of sweep back and dihedral angle converts the off center weight into a bank, as the plane starts to react to the skid. Again, the pilot must yaw the nose up to continue the bank or it will drop into a spiral dive.

Some ultralights use tip spoilers or rudders to drag a wing back. This creates a roll by increasing the lift on the wing swinging forward and decreasing it on the wing being pulled back by the control device. Again, the nose must be pitched up either by an elevator in front of the wing or behind and, in some cases, by having the pilot move back to shift the center of gravity aft.

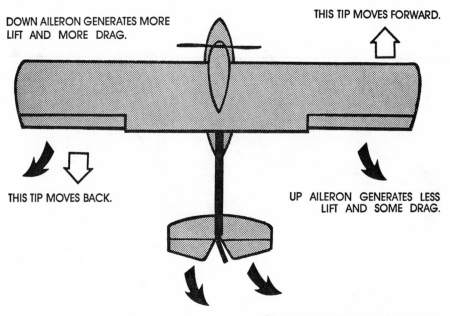

DOWN AILERON GENERATES MORE LIFT AND MORE DRAG.

THIS TIP MOVES FORWARD.

THIS TIP MOVES BACK.

UP AILERON GENERATES LESS LIFT AND SOME DRAG.

RUDDER COUNTERACTS THE ADVERSE AILERON YAW, KEEPING TURN COORDINATED.

Fig. 1-4. The rudder is used to balance the adverse yaw created by the ailerons.

Slip and Skid Indicators

The best way to tell if your ultralight is being properly turned is to put a string in front of you, or a ball in a curved glass tube filled with oil. The simplest is the string tied out in front. It will be streaming straight back at your nose when the plane is being flown correctly. The yaw string must not be in the propeller blast, which works out nicely in a pusher. If the propeller is in front, there's no easy place to put a yaw string, so the conventional ball-in-tube slip indicator, as used by regular planes, can be mounted anywhere in front of you.

How to Use the Indicators

The actions of the yaw string and ball are opposite to one another. In a turn, if the yaw string is pointing toward the outside the ball would be on the inside of the turn. Both would show the plane slipping toward the center of the turn.

In airplanes with rudder controls, the rule is to "step-on-the-ball." In the case just mentioned, that means the pilot would push on the rudder to the inside of the turn and ease the stick back. This would swing the tail around, centering the ball, as well as the string. For the yaw string, I "push-it-back-with-the-stick." In the above example, the ball and string could both be centered by moving the stick left and the rudder right. The movements of the stick and rudder in a conventional

18

airplane are coordinated, so no matter if the rudder is used for stepping on the ball or the stick is used to pull the string over, they should both move together.

In a weight shift ultralight, if the string is streaming to the outside of the turn, you are slipping. This can be corrected by pushing out harder on the bar and moving outside, i.e., shifting your weight outside and back. Conversely, if the string

AS THE PLANE FLIES, IT DEFLECTS AIR DOWNWARD FOR LIFT.

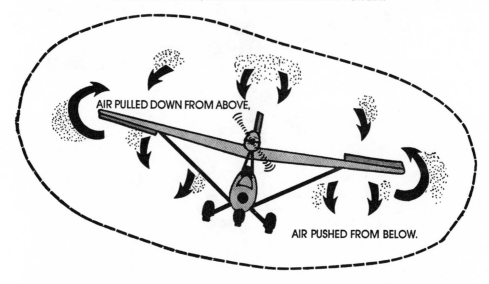

AIR PULLED DOWN FROM ABOVE,

AIR PUSHED FROM BELOW.

Fig. 1-5. The "Apparent Mass Effect" says that the entire mass of air affected by the wing must be rolled, as well as the mass of the aircraft.

is streaming toward the inside of the turn, it means you are skidding. Correct by bringing down the nose and/or increasing the bank. Changes in bank angle and pitch should be coordinated, the same as with the stick and rudder of conventional controls. If a weight shift ultralight uses a ball indicator, the rule is to move your weight opposite the ball. If the ball is to the right, move to the left and vice versa. Again, pitch should be changed with fore and aft weight shift. If you are turning and the ball rolls to the inside, you should move your weight to the opposite side while smoothly pitching up at the same time.

Continuous Circling

When a plane is rolled into a turn, the outer wing will have more lift than the inner wing. If no other movement to the controls, or weight shift, is made, the plane will spiral dive! The airspeed difference between the wing tip speeding around the outside of the circle, and the slower pivoting inside tip, will increase the bank. The pilot must stop this increasing roll in order to make a steady circle. With weight shift, it may mean the pilot has to "high-side" the bar. The extra weight to the outside compensates for the greater lift.

In a conventionally controlled ultralight, once the desired bank angle is achieved, the stick should be moved to the outside of the turn. The inner wing now has down aileron and the outer wing has up aileron, compensating for the differences in lift. The pilot must also hold rudder to the inside of the turn to compensate for yaw.

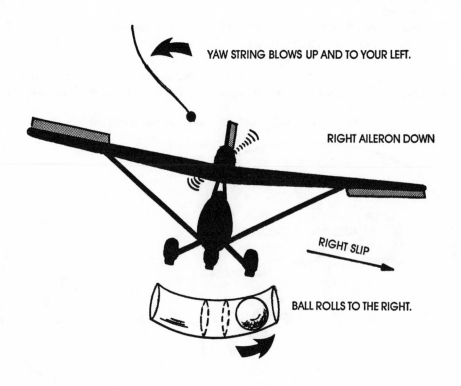

YAW STRING BLOWS UP AND TO YOUR LEFT.

RIGHT AILERON DOWN

RIGHT SLIP

BALL ROLLS TO THE RIGHT.

TO CORRECT, BRING STICK LEFT AND BACK SOME WHILE PUSHING RIGHT RUDDER.

IN A WEIGHT SHIFT ULTRALIGHT, PUSH THE BAR TO THE RIGHT AND OUT SOME, MOVING WEIGHT LEFT AND BACK.

Fig. 1-6. This is what happens in a slip to the right.

This is a "crossed-control" situation, but the string or ball will be exactly centered, and the turn coordinated.

With the weight shift or conventionally controlled airplane in a slow turn, "crossed-controls" condition, there is danger of spinning because the inner wing is going so much slower. If the plane starts to rotate with the inner wing dropping further, the back pressure on the stick should quickly be released, or the weight moved forward by pulling on the bar. The angle of attack must be reduced! The bank angle should not be changed if you want to keep the same, round circle. Round circles are very important to precision flying.

As a pilot becomes more practiced and familiar with the airplane, it will become very natural to fly in slow, steep turns without skidding or slipping, and using subtle pitch downs to stop the beginnings of a stall.

You should be aware of your airspeed at all times during turns so you know when to get the nose down. The steeper the bank and more quickly the plane goes around, the more the G loading will be increased. A higher loading raises the stalling speed. The quicker you plan to turn, the more you must let the speed build up, before entering the turn.

Airspeed or Angle of Attack

I emphasize airspeed instead of angle of attack in discussions of flying in gusts and turning in wind gradients. Some fliers insist that angle of attack should be stressed. They say, if you never exceed the stalling angle of attack of your wing, regardless of speed, you'll never stall. True, the stalling angle of any airfoil is the same no matter what the airspeed! You can stall at maximum speed as well as at minimum speed going straight up or straight down. If the wing is pitched past its stalling angle, it will stall. Yet, stating, "Never exceed the stalling angle," is almost equal to saying, "Never crash." It doesn't tell the pilot anything practical. Airspeed is most important.

Here's why. Lift is generated as the square of the speed. At high speed, the plane is flying at a low angle of attack. At high speed, to exceed the stall angle of your wing, you must pitch it to such an extent that the G loads would be immediately felt and you would be definitely doing something with the controls. The visual change in pitch angle to reach the stall would be dramatic enough that it would take a very insensitive pilot to not notice what's happening. Your chances of inadvertantly stalling at cruising speed are remote, and recovery is instantaneous when nosed down.

Fig. 1-7. At cruising speed or higher, the wing must be pitched-up radically to make it stall. Any pilot would notice the change in pitch angle and G-loading.

21

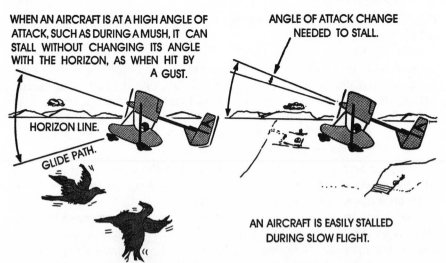

WHEN AN AIRCRAFT IS AT A HIGH ANGLE OF ATTACK, SUCH AS DURING A MUSH, IT CAN STALL WITHOUT CHANGING ITS ANGLE WITH THE HORIZON, AS WHEN HIT BY A GUST.

ANGLE OF ATTACK CHANGE NEEDED TO STALL.

HORIZON LINE.

GLIDE PATH.

AN AIRCRAFT IS EASILY STALLED DURING SLOW FLIGHT.

Fig. 1-8. Maintenance of proper airspeed is most important to keep from stalling. Watch your airspeed indicator, as it is your best tool for keeping the wing from stalling.

Now take the case of flying very slowly. To develop the downwash needed to keep the plane up at low speed, means the wing is at a high angle of attack. Without the slightest visual change in the pitch of the airplane or movement of any control, a stall can occur if a gust from the rear hits one wing, the plane flies into an upcurrent, or the engine loses power. As the plane sinks, the angle of attack increases further still. The pilot cannot really tell tne angle of attack because it may be different on each wing. For example, in a descending turn the inner wing has a higher angle of attack than the outer and may stall, even though both wings may appear to have the same angle.

Any aviator can inadvertantly exceed the stalling angle of the wing because there's no definite way to see what it is. Is it possible to fit the ultralight with some kind of device to tell the true angle of attack? Why not tie a string on the lift wires and look at the strings to compare their angles with that of the wing? Or, why not mount a little vane on a vertical board with lines drawn to show the stalling angle? Well, none of these ideas work because the air around the airplane is deflected by the wing at the same angle, so there is little difference in the angle of the markers and the wing itself.

You must put two indicators extending about one chord length, say 4 feet, on each wing tip with the indicating vanes large enough to see at that distance. Of course, it could also be done with electronic pickups and remote sensing devices connected to an indicator in front of the pilot. Perhaps some pilots could be made safer by such an angle of attack indicator, but it is only one clue to the total dynamics of the plane. Airspeed is far easier to use. The stalling speed, as shown on the airspeed, will never vary if the plane is at the same weight and G loading. Only if the plane is heavier or if G's are pulled, as in a turn, will the stall speed be higher. By the "airspeed," is meant being aware by looking at the airspeed indicator itself, sensing the wind flow past the plane, the feel of the controls, sounds of the boundary layer and, in fact, everything except the relative movement of the ground.

Remember, low airspeed warns that you're in an area of possible stall by inadvertant angle of attack changes caused by gusts, increased G loading, or by slowing.

22

THE AIRSPEED INDICATOR IS THE MOST IMPORTANT GAUGE ON STALLING, BUT SOME PILOTS MAY ENJOY CHECKING THE ANGLE OF ATTACK UNDER VARIOUS CONDITIONS — SUCH AS DURING PULL-OUTS, HIGH AND LOW SPEEDS, DIFFERENT BANK ANGLES (G-LOADS), ETC.

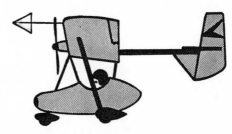

MOUNT A COUPLE OF FEET AHEAD OF THE WING, ON EACH TIP (ONE WING WILL OFTEN STALL BEFORE THE OTHER).

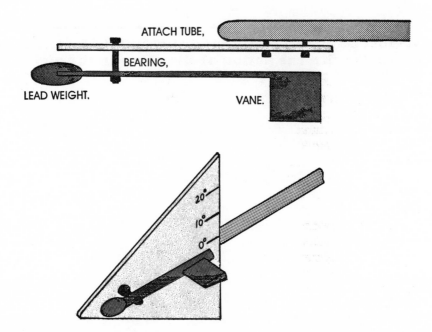

MARK ANGLES AND FLIGHT TEST TO CALIBRATE THE STALL.   A WING WILL ALWAYS STALL AT THE SAME ANGLE OF ATTACK, REGARDLESS OF AIRSPEED!

Fig. 1-9. The angle of attack indicator.

Summary of the Basics of Turning Flight

- You must bank to turn.
- A sharper turn needs more bank and speed.
- Roll, and pitch nose up together.
- Yaw string right needs left rudder and right stick to correct.
- Ball to the right needs right rudder and left stick to correct.
- Slipping inward to the turn needs reduced bank and nose up to correct.
- Skidding outward to the turn needs increased bank and nose down to correct.
- Crossed controls and nose up are needed for a steady circle of 360°.
- Airspeed is most important to prevent inadvertant stalls.

"It must be understood that ground speed has nothing to do with the action of the plane in the air!"

Chapter Two~ Flying in the Wind

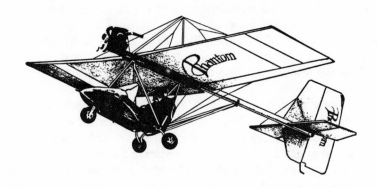

Flying in the Wind

With understanding and practice, there's no reason ultralights can't be flown in winds equal to their stalling speeds, or even more. At the University of Illinois, where I was a member of the Glider Club, we often flew in 40 mph winds with a glider that stalled at 32 mph. We found it challenging and great fun turning after release from the tow car, watching the ground whipping by as we flew downwind, and then turning into the wind to land almost like a helicopter.

We had not a single accident due to winds in many hundreds of flights. One time, during a meet with the Purdue Glider Club, we were using their winch to tow us. It was so windy that day in Lafayette, Indiana, we could tow the glider up into the stronger wind gradient then stop the motor and slowly pay out the line. The 250 pound glider would kite higher and higher as it climbed on the outreeling line. I suppose it took a lot of skill and judgment to fly in those conditions or perhaps we just didn't know any better.

To get the most out of your ultralight as well as to be a better pilot, learn to fly in the wind. You never know when the wind may come up while you're flying!

On the Ground

Ultralights can easily be blown over if not properly tied down. Concentrate on keeping the wings out of a lifting attitude. If the wind gets under the wings, few tie downs are strong enough to hold the pull of what could be well over a thousand pounds, which would be generated in a 30 mph wind against an ultralight wing at a high angle of attack. When winds are this strong, the tail should be lifted high so

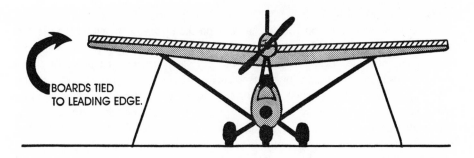

BOARDS TIED
TO LEADING EDGE.

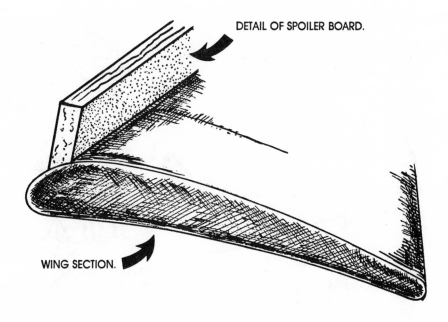

DETAIL OF SPOILER BOARD.

WING SECTION.

Fig. 2-1. "Spoiler boards" can be attached to the wing leading edges to protect the aircraft during a wind, by preventing the generation of lift.

the wind pushes slightly on the top of the wing. It might be necessary to stand by the tail in order to lift it quickly or swing the plane around to keep the wing at a negative angle to the wind. The plane should be faced into the wind with the nose low instead of with the trailing edge to the wing. The rear of the wing is not as strong as the front and can be bent or broken more easily from a strong gust.

Spoilers, made of slats tied or wired to the top of the leading edge, reduce lift drastically by disturbing the smooth flow of air over the wings. They could be made like a small snow fence and rolled up after use.

The wings should be partially collapsed, if possible, when you plan to leave the ship alone. On a trike, take the wing off and fold the control bar so the wing can be tied down low to the ground where the wind is much less.

Takeoff in the Wind

One person should be on the tail and one on the upwind wing while the plane is taxiing. The pilot should be ready for takeoff before the helpers let go. When the plane takes off, the angle of climb will be very steep because the plane flies into ever increasing wind, which provides free energy. This is wonderful, except a windy day is also often gusty. If, when climbing steeply the wind drops, the plane will lose speed very quickly and may stall, if the pilot is not fast enough in nosing down. The stall due to a sudden decrease in headwind is very difficult to detect. The pilot has not changed his angle of attack and the plane may be climbing with good airspeed when it suddenly begins dropping. As it falls, even though the pilot is still holding the same nose position, the angle of attack will increase since the air is hitting the wing more from below. Then, as if that's not bad enough, the plane is settling into the slower moving air near the ground, making the speed relative to the air even less.

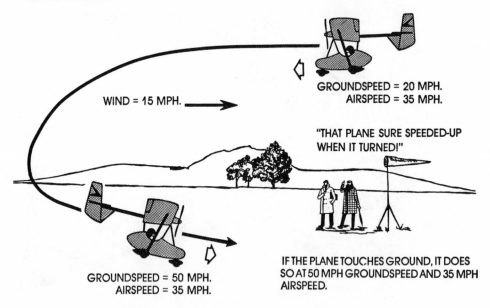

GROUNDSPEED = 20 MPH.
AIRSPEED = 35 MPH.

WIND = 15 MPH.

"THAT PLANE SURE SPEEDED-UP WHEN IT TURNED!"

GROUNDSPEED = 50 MPH.
AIRSPEED = 35 MPH.

IF THE PLANE TOUCHES GROUND, IT DOES SO AT 50 MPH GROUNDSPEED AND 35 MPH AIRSPEED.

FIG. 2-2. A tailwind adds to groundspeed only — not airspeed!

Few pilots who have not stalled in a wind gradient can imagine how quickly and radically the ship must be recovered with a quick dive and pull out in the last few feet. Some recommend keeping the speed up in windy weather during climbout which is okay, but the focus of this book is to encourage the highest level of pilotage and performance with the safest techniques.

To achieve the very best angle of climb in clearing obstacles in the least space, the wind gradient can be used by climbing at a speed very close to the stall. Going faster degrades the climb because most ultralights are high drag machines. The drag goes up very quickly as the speed increases, leaving much less power for climb. In gusty winds an ultralight going 10 mph faster than its best climb speed will have a greater margin above stall speed, but the climb is so much less, that full performance will be well below that of a plane flying slowly.

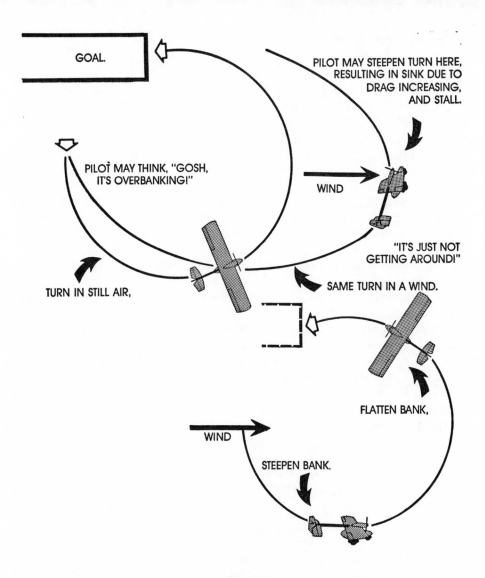

GOAL.

PILOT MAY STEEPEN TURN HERE, RESULTING IN SINK DUE TO DRAG INCREASING, AND STALL.

PILOT MAY THINK, "GOSH, IT'S OVERBANKING!"

WIND

"IT'S JUST NOT GETTING AROUND!"

TURN IN STILL AIR,

SAME TURN IN A WIND.

FLATTEN BANK,

STEEPEN BANK.

WIND

TO MAKE A CIRCULAR PATH OVER THE GROUND WHILE IN A WIND, THE PILOT MUST STEEPEN THE BANK DOWNWIND AND FLATTEN THE BANK AS HE PROCEEDS UPWIND. IF THERE IS A WIND GRADIENT, IT WOULD HELP SUCH A MANEUVER.

Fig. 2-3. Problems of a downwind turn, not caused by the wind gradient.

A pilot must be very aware of his speed and the feel of his plane, to be ready at the first instant of power loss or wind slowing, to drop the nose quickly. An ultralight is much safer than most planes because recovery from a stall takes only a few yards as a result of its low wing loading. As a pilot becomes more experienced, the plane can be gradually brought down to the best angle of climb. I find that my "own minimum" flying speed in a plane goes down 5 to 10 mph after a few hours practice because I can sense the stall more subconsciously.

The "Optical" Gradient

It is important in ultralight flying to understand the confusions brought about by turning in the wind at low altitude. Have you ever been in a 360 degree movie dome — the kind that gives such a real feeling of being immersed in the scene? The movie will often show a drive along a mountain road. In the darkened theater people "Oh and Ah" as they sway "against" the curves.

Our eyes are the major sense to interpret relative motion. Sure, we have the semi-circular canals in the ear that sense movement, but they do not override the eyes. In fact, we can become nauseated when our eyes tell a different story of motion.

Birds seem to have built-in ways of sensing their rate of climb and sink, as well as direction. We are however, creatures of the ground and are not equipped, neither through evolution nor ground based experience, to deal with the three dimensional world of the air without special training and instruments.

Ultralights, gliders and hang gliders fly slowly in relation to the wind and often turn low, so we cue our actions by reference to the ground. This is often confusing. Approach to landing accidents such as spins, stalls, and hitting a wing are the major category of mishaps.

In the early days of flying, when everyone stayed low, pilots found their airplanes seemed to handle differently, depending on wether they were turning into the wind or downwind. It was observed that if a pilot were flying "against-the-wind," and turned to fly with the wind, the plane would drop, sometimes even hitting the ground. If a pilot turned toward the wind after flying downwind, the plane was "harder" to turn and easily gained altitude. It was obvious something must be happening because of the wind direction. Let's examine this "problem" in detail.

Fig. 2-4. Always keep the yaw string centered during normal flight.

30

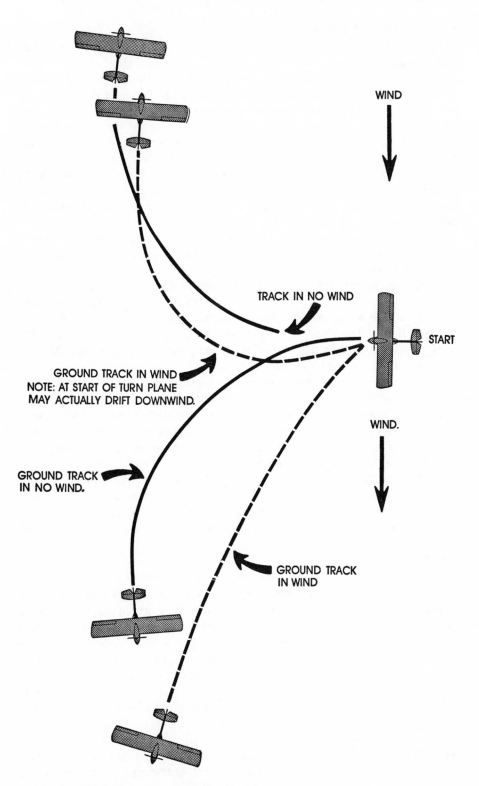

WIND

TRACK IN NO WIND

START

GROUND TRACK IN WIND
NOTE: AT START OF TURN PLANE
MAY ACTUALLY DRIFT DOWNWIND.

WIND.

GROUND TRACK
IN NO WIND.

GROUND TRACK
IN WIND

Fig. 2-5. Turns upwind compared to turns downwind.

31

The Acceleration Theory

One explanation, which I call the "Inertial Acceleration Theory," goes like this: Suppose you are flying 35 mph into a 15 mph wind. Here, of course, your ground speed is 20 mph (35 mph flying speed minus the 15 mph headwind). When you turn downwind, ground speed increases from 20 to 50 mph (35 plus 15)! To increase the speed of you and your airplane from 20 to 50 mph required energy which can only come from losing altitude, thus turning the potential energy of height into the kinetic energy of speed. This sinking, explained the theory, is the danger of downwind turns. Pilots were cautioned to have extra speed and use special care to be a good distance away from the ground when making a downwind turn. In the same way, turning upwind resulted in a gain of energy as the ground speed slowed from 50 mph to 20 mph, enabling the plane to climb. The idea took hold because it seemed to square with our observations.

But, when planes began to fly higher, the phenomenon magically disappeared. If an aircraft at high altitude is made to perform circles in a strong wind, pilots could find no change in air speed or altitude!

Arguments raged on in print and at "hangar flying" sessions. High flyers reasoned an airplane is flying in the air at 35 mph no matter if its going into the wind or with the wind, its speed over the ground making no difference. "Oh, yea?" said the "Inertial Theorists." "Then how about a downwind landing across a ditch at 50 mph, compared to one upwind when the plane would hit at only 20 mph. Don't tell us ground speed isn't real."

To those trained in physics, however, the explanation is elementary. When the plane is in the air, the ground is not in the same system of reference. Ground speed, in fact, does not make the slightest difference in the aircraft's inertia. Of course, if the plane touches the ground, how fast the plane is going in reference to the ground *is* important because the ground is now part of the system. Fortunately, the Inertial Theory was put to rest many years ago.

Nevertheless, a nagging doubt troubled even those flyers who found no changes in speed or altitude circling in the wind up high. When turns are done at low altitude, the plane seemed to handle differently as well as drop when turning downwind, even though they knew the changes in ground speed had no affect.

The Wind Gradient

It was found that the wind is slower near the ground, because of the drag of grass, bushes, and a rough surface texture. "Aha," said pilots who found their airplanes dropping when they turned downwind. They argued that when turning downwind the lower wing dips into the slower air, while the upper wing is in faster air. This tips the plane over more and, thus, it is more easily thrown to the ground. Conversely, in turning upwind, the pilot must push harder on the controls, whether weight shift or control levers, to get the plane turned.

Here there seems to be disagreement, because some say exactly the opposite will happen. They say the lower wing, extending down into the slower air, is actually going faster and would tend to right itself because of its greater lift. When turning upwind, they say, the lower wing is, in fact, moving relatively slower than the upper wing so the plane should tend to roll into an upwind turn.

This is exactly right concerning relative speeds, but ignored is the difference in angle of attack between the wings when performing turns in a wind gradient.

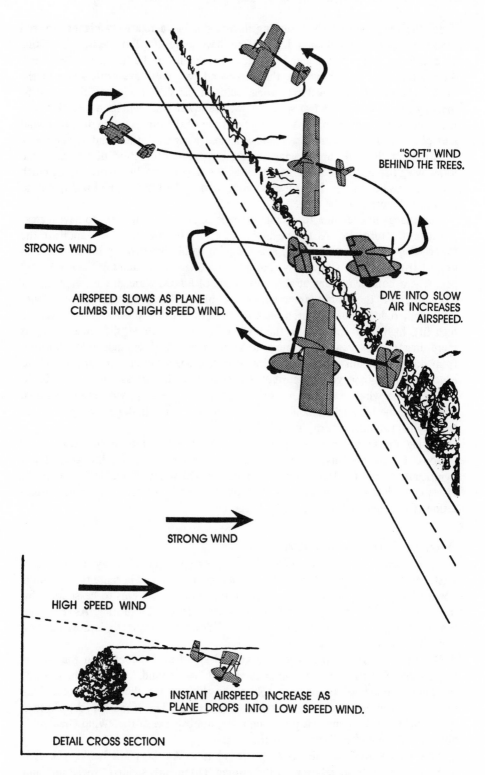

"SOFT" WIND
BEHIND THE TREES.

STRONG WIND

AIRSPEED SLOWS AS PLANE
CLIMBS INTO HIGH SPEED WIND.

DIVE INTO SLOW
AIR INCREASES
AIRSPEED.

STRONG WIND

HIGH SPEED WIND

INSTANT AIRSPEED INCREASE AS
PLANE DROPS INTO LOW SPEED WIND.

DETAIL CROSS SECTION

Fig. 2-6. Possible technique for albatross-like wind gradient dynamic soaring.

33

True, the lower wing, when turning downwind, has a relatively higher airspeed than the upper wing and should, therefore, have more lift. Trouble is, it is striking air at a lower angle of attack and therefore, has less lift in the first part of the turn. As the turn continues however, the downwind part will have both wings at the same angle of attack. The lower wing, being in the slower wind gradient, will be meeting the air at a greater airspeed. Now, the lower wing will have more lift than the upper wing and the plane will try to roll out of the turn. During the cross wind part of the turn, the lower wing will have a greater angle of attack and will continue to lift more than the upper wing. In the upwind continuation of the turn, the lower wing has the same angle of attack as the upper wing but is now going much slower relative to the air. It has less lift compared to the top wing and will therefore tend to roll more into the turn.

The change in drag due to change in angle of attack would seem to have a great affect on the turn also. At the beginning of a turn to downwind in a gradient, the lower wing would have less drag, and the pilot would have to use more rudder to keep it from slipping. Conversely, the pilot would use less rudder in the downwind part where both wings are at the same angle of attack. Here, the lower wing has more lift, and thus more drag, tending to pull it back. As the turn continues crosswind, rudder must be used against the turn because the lower wing is in a high lift, high drag position. In the upwind part of the circle, the lower wing has more drag, causing yaw, which must be counteracted with enough rudder to keep from skidding. If this sounds complicated and, if one set of circumstances tends to cancel out the other, you are correct. The strength of the winds, the angle of bank, length of the wings, variation of the gradient over the span, yaw and directional stability of the ultralight are all infinitely variable factors in determining what will actually happen during turns in a wind gradient.

Having measured this "Wind Gradient" over fairly smooth surfaces and at hilltops, I find the change in wind speed over distance from the ground not significant enough to effect turning as much as pilots may think. Yes, of course, it exists but it just isn't the cause of the problem. More important is our misinterpretation of the relative movement of the ground.

Downwind and Upwind Turns

Let's examine what your brain tells you in an upwind turn say, to the right. First, as you fly downwind, it seems you are going very fast because the ground is flowing by quickly. When you begin the turn, the ground seems to be slipping by from the right too much and the plane doesn't seem to be turning. As the plane keeps "sliding" sideways, it appears to be "slowing" because it is now heading upwind and has less *ground speed*.

Our brain interprets the change in ground speed as a reduction in the rate of turn so the pilot tries to turn harder to make it "get around." Close to the ground, the pilot is reluctant to bank steeply so he skids to get the nose around. This situation can easily result in the lower wing stalling. The plane can drop into a spin or the lower wing may hit the ground. No, not because of the "Wind Gradient," but due to the mind misinterpreting the cues.

Now let's analyze the dreaded downwind turn. As the plane banks, the turn seems to accelerate in relation to the ground. Often, this sudden "speed-up" and quick approach to our goal, gives the impression that the plane is very "easy" to

THE AIRCRAFT MOVES SO QUICKLY AND OVERRUNS THE GOAL IN SUCH A WAY THAT THE PILOT OFTEN INCORRECTLY SLOWS THE AIRCRAFT AND MAY INCORRECTLY TIGHTEN THE TURN, AS WELL.

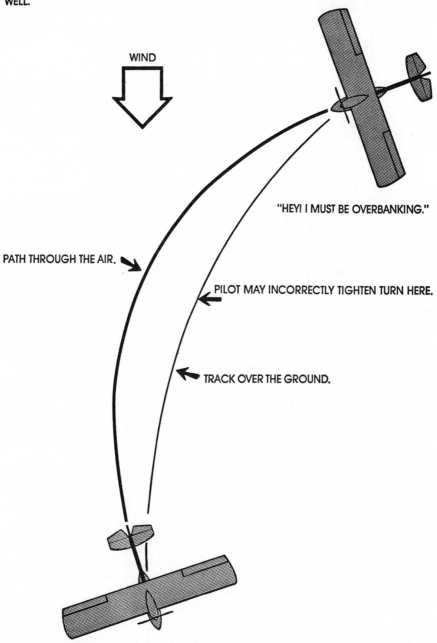

Fig. 2-7. The confusion of a downwind turn.

turn. In fact, if made with the normal control pressures and movement, it seems to be overbanking. You may subconsciously slow the plane and reduce the bank, but the plane slides too far away from its intended point. Now you must bank **very**

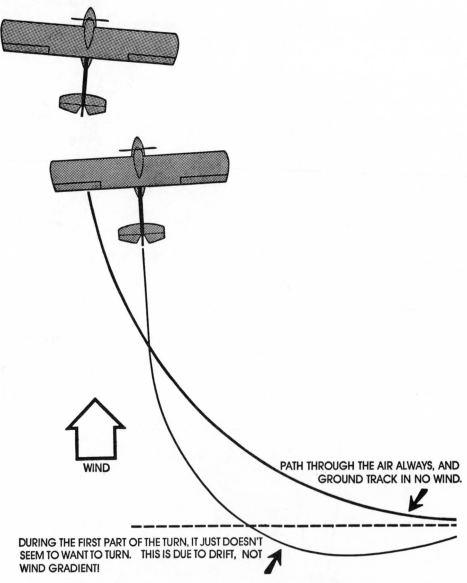

WIND

PATH THROUGH THE AIR ALWAYS, AND GROUND TRACK IN NO WIND.

DURING THE FIRST PART OF THE TURN, IT JUST DOESN'T SEEM TO WANT TO TURN. THIS IS DUE TO DRIFT, NOT WIND GRADIENT!

Fig. 2-8. Variations in air track and ground track in making an upwind turn from a crosswind.

steeply to tighten the turn to get it around to reach your goal. Low over the ground, when it seems the plane is banking too much, you tend to skid it around instead of properly banking more steeply.

Discussions of low turns recommend speed to counter the "mysterious" affects of the downwind turn. This is poor advice. An aircraft should always be flown at the optimum speed for the performance desired. I have seen airplanes smashed against the ground going sideways out of control but with plenty of airspeed. Simply saying "don't stall," is meaningless.

Don't Look at the Ground

The best way to deal with flying low in the wind is: (1) accept the fact that we aren't equipped to handle the situation, just as we are unable to fly in clouds using our senses, without special instruments; (2) Select your goal, such as the edge of the landing spot. Begin a turn that you judge, from experience, will be the proper angle of bank to reach the goal. Concentrate on the airspeed and on keeping the plane from slipping or skidding. (3) Look out at the ground momentarily only.

Glances should be so brief that the movement of the ground does not confuse the brain. Eyes should be looking far out at the horizon and the instruments only. A good way to practice is to do 360 degree turns in a strong wind at 500 feet without looking out. Then, try to do it looking at the ground. When you look back in, the plane is usually too fast or slow and in a slip or skid.

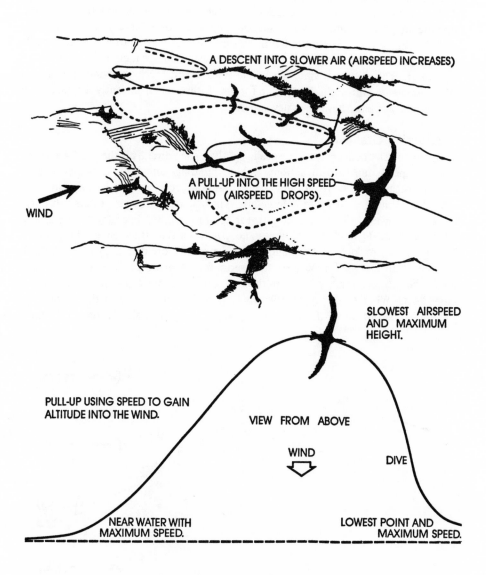

Fig. 2-9. How the albatross soars in a wind gradient.

37

The Perfect Gradient

A wind gradient does exist very close to the ground, of course, and an albatross, in fact, soars in it. This is called dynamic soaring which is done by diving with the wind into the low speed air near the surface of the ocean and building up airspeed to do a quick turn and climb back into the wind. The increasing wind with height equals its loss in speed as it pulls up, so the bird is able to climb enough to repeat the maneuver and fly thousands of miles without flapping. Should we pull up into the wind to make use of the wind gradient? It would certainly work in some cases and once a safe enough height is reached, to be sure of a stall recovery distance, a pull up would allow the plane to make use of the faster windspeed with height.

It doesn't seem possible to duplicate the performance of the Albatross however, because the wind gradient is too shallow and weak over land. These birds fly in the "roaring forties" in the southern hemisphere where 40 knot winds are the rule and the gradient is sharply defined over the ocean. Perhaps it could be done over a row of trees in a strong wind, where the trees would block the wind and make a sharp gradient. But we'll leave that for the future when instantly turning, very streamlined airplanes have been developed.

Obstruction Gradient

An important concern to low speed, lightly loaded aircraft is the sudden change in wind speed due to obstructions. Behind buildings and hills, it can be unpredictable because air swirls around, behind solid objects. Fences, bushes and trees slow the air more evenly and completely. Why? Some of the air "filters" through the object, instead allowing a large rotor to form, while increasing the drag. Try hitting a "Whiffle Ball" full of holes and you'll see the effect. Similarly, a lot of little branches, making up trees and bushes, have far more drag than a solid wall. It has been well known for decades that snow fences made of slats spaced a little ways apart, to let some of the air through, are far more effective in controlling snow drifts. What to do? Again, like turning in the wind, some of the problem is real and some optical. High up, it seems you are going more slowly than down low,

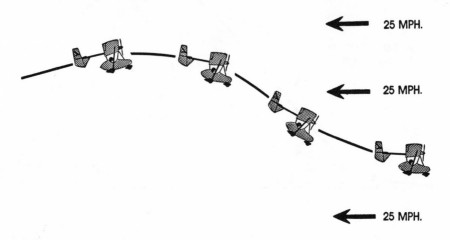

25 MPH.

25 MPH.

25 MPH.

Fig. 2-10. A stall and recovery at altitude.

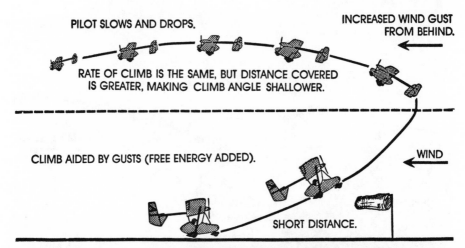

PILOT SLOWS AND DROPS.

INCREASED WIND GUST FROM BEHIND.

RATE OF CLIMB IS THE SAME, BUT DISTANCE COVERED IS GREATER, MAKING CLIMB ANGLE SHALLOWER.

CLIMB AIDED BY GUSTS (FREE ENERGY ADDED).

WIND

SHORT DISTANCE.

ALTHOUGH THE CLIMB MAY BE IDENTICAL IN RATE, IT SEEMS LOWER BECAUSE THE ULTRALIGHT COVERS SO MUCH DISTANCE PER UNIT HEIGHT GAINED — WHEN GOING DOWNWIND. GUSTS MAY ACTUALLY DETRACT FROM CLIMB DOWNWIND. WATCH THE AIRSPEED INDICATOR AND CLIMB AT BEST RATE SPEED. IGNORE THE ILLUSION CREATED BY THE GROUND.

Fig. 2-11. The confusion of why it seems so hard to climb after a downwind turn after takeoff.

because you are farther away from the ground. Even with no wind, the tendency down low would be to slow down because the ground appears to be going faster as you descend. If the plane is slowed to what seems normal at 100 feet, it may begin mushing or even stalling at 10 feet. Combined with a wind strong enough to create a gradient, the effect can be even more serious. Prepare to dive as you approach a field surrounded by plants or buildings. Watch the air speed and be ready for instant corrections.

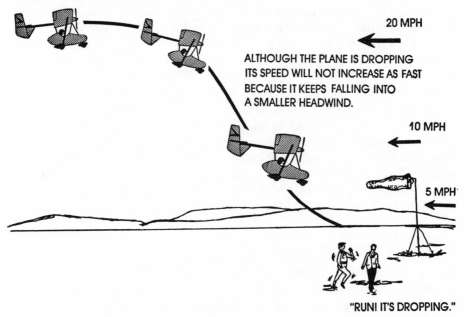

20 MPH

ALTHOUGH THE PLANE IS DROPPING ITS SPEED WILL NOT INCREASE AS FAST BECAUSE IT KEEPS FALLING INTO A SMALLER HEADWIND.

10 MPH

5 MPH

"RUN! IT'S DROPPING."

Fig. 2-12. A stall and recovery (maybe) at low altitude in a wind gradient.

39

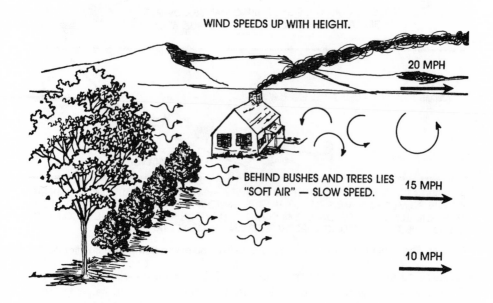

WIND = 25 MPH

WIND SPEEDS UP WITH HEIGHT.

20 MPH

BEHIND BUSHES AND TREES LIES "SOFT AIR" — SLOW SPEED.

15 MPH

10 MPH

Fig. 2-13. Obstruction gradients vary, depending on the type of object blocking the wind.

Low turns are fun. The sense of motion and the thrill of flying is enhanced close to the ground. Our skills as pilots are more called upon in such maneuvers. In winds, low turns are more dangerous and the margin for error is small. We may tend to concentrate on the ground sliding by and become confused by the wind drift. Hitting the ground going downwind will cause many times more damage than upwind because the energy produced goes up as the square of the speed. A crash at 40 mph has four times the energy of a crash at 20 mph!

Climbing after a takeoff and turning downwind reduces the climb angle, but not the climb rate, because you cover more ground in the climb. However, if there is a wind gradient, the climb rate will be less as well because the ultralight will keep on climbing into stronger tailwinds which reduce the airspeed. So, unless there is a good reason, such as obstacles upwind, it is better to climb into the wind until well above the gradient, before turning downwind. By understanding what is happening when flying in the wind, a thoughtful pilot will minimize the dangers.

Crosswind Takeoffs

Ultralights takeoff and land in such a small space, and fly from fields in which there is no particular runway, that crosswinds are often not a problem when compared to conventional aircraft that must use paved runways. This is fortunate because the low wing loading of an ultralight makes it very sensitive to crosswinds. A normal afternoon wind of 12 mph is almost half the takeoff speed of an ultralight! A jet landing at 120 mph in a 60 mph crosswind would put its pilot at the

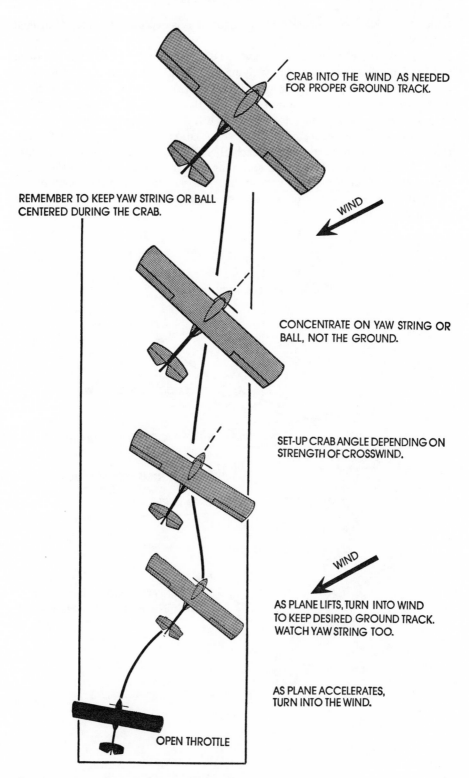

CRAB INTO THE WIND AS NEEDED FOR PROPER GROUND TRACK.

REMEMBER TO KEEP YAW STRING OR BALL CENTERED DURING THE CRAB.

WIND

CONCENTRATE ON YAW STRING OR BALL, NOT THE GROUND.

SET-UP CRAB ANGLE DEPENDING ON STRENGTH OF CROSSWIND.

WIND

AS PLANE LIFTS, TURN INTO WIND TO KEEP DESIRED GROUND TRACK. WATCH YAW STRING TOO.

AS PLANE ACCELERATES, TURN INTO THE WIND.

OPEN THROTTLE

Fig. 2-14. An example of a crosswind takeoff.

41

limit of his skill. So too would an ultralight, if it is necessary to take off or land in a crosswind.

In the air, the plane does not care which direction the wind is moving, but there is a brief moment when it is almost flying but not off the ground. In a cross wind, the landing gear may be going one direction with the wings and tail going in another. At the beginning of a crosswind run, the surfaces of the plane are sliding through the air sideways and, as it begins to lift, the wheels skid sideways. To cope with this confusing and often destructive situation, it is best to begin the run crosswind. As the plane begins to reach flying speed, swing across the "runway" part of your flying field so you are going directly into the wind as the speed picks up. When the plane lifts, turn so the plane will crab along the length of the flying field until it is clear of surrounding obstacles, then climb directly into the wind if you wish.

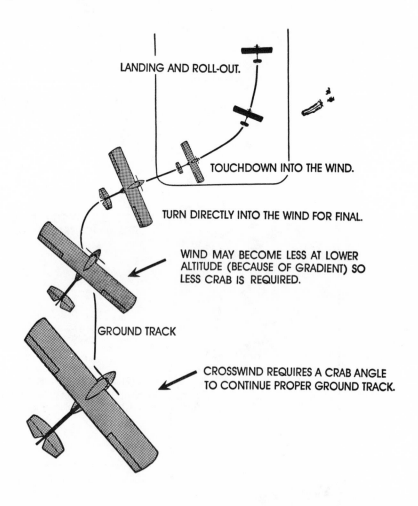

LANDING AND ROLL-OUT.

TOUCHDOWN INTO THE WIND.

TURN DIRECTLY INTO THE WIND FOR FINAL.

WIND MAY BECOME LESS AT LOWER ALTITUDE (BECAUSE OF GRADIENT) SO LESS CRAB IS REQUIRED.

GROUND TRACK

CROSSWIND REQUIRES A CRAB ANGLE TO CONTINUE PROPER GROUND TRACK.

Fig. 2-15. A typical sequence for a crosswind landing.

Crosswind Landings

Almost as controversial as the downwind turn is the technique for handling crosswind landings. Many pilots say the slip is best. A slipping approach is one in which the nose is aimed the way you wish to go while the wing is held into the wind so the plane slides sideways. To keep the airplane from turning into the wind, because its natural stability forces the nose in the direction of the slip, the rudder must be held opposite to keep the nose going straight. Just before the plane touches down, it is leveled so that the wing tip does not hit the ground.

Some ultralights cannot do a slip landing because the wing banking and rudder controls are interconnected, making the plane turn automatically. Others have no provision for holding the plane in a slip with crossed controls. Furthermore, some ultralights have no separate banking controls at all!

Crabbing

Ultralight pilots should learn to make crab type crosswind approaches and landings instead of the slip.

Why fly a plane crosswise in the air to make it go straight? Slipping always hurts performance. It should certainly not be done during a climbout in a crosswind,

A CROSSWIND OCCURS WHENEVER THE AIR IS MOVING IN A DIRECTION DIFFERENT THAN THE INTENDED COURSE. TO MAINTAIN A DESIRED COURSE, THE AIRCRAFT MUST HEAD INTO THE CROSSWIND — THE FASTER THE CROSSWIND, THE MORE THE AIRCRAFT MUST POINT INTO IT. A CROSSWIND IS COMPENSATED FOR BY "CRABBING".

THE MOVEMENT OF AN AIR MASS IS CALLED WIND.

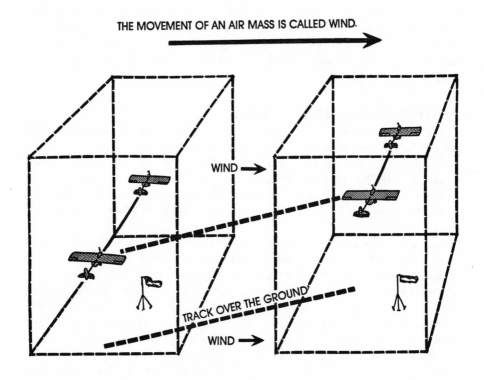

Fig. 2-16. Understanding flight in a crosswind.

43

because the rate of climb could be considerably less due to the extra drag of going sideways. During cross countries, slope soaring, or flying around the field, there's no need to slide sideways to go in the direction you want. Your plane should always be flown with the air passing directly over the nose to the tail for efficiency as well as safety. The best way to handle crosswinds is by crabbing; that is, its path through the air is angled to counteract its drift over the ground. The combination of wind drift and heading makes the path over the ground whatever you wish. It takes some skill because you have to look out the side in the direction you're going, with the nose pointed into the wind at a different heading. Flying toward a goal, back and forth in a crosswind, is good practice for the time you may need to land downwind. A very slow ultralight in a strong crosswind is best landed across the runway, because the plane is down and stopped very quickly there's no need for a long landing roll. But, if the approach must be flown crosswind, the plane should be angled into the wind while you look out the side at the runway, making sure your body is heading directly to the touchdown spot. If the plane is drifting to one side of the runway, bank opposite to the drift to make a small turn toward the wind, while leveling the wings. Check again to see if the drift is continuing. For example, if the plane is moving into the wind, bank away a bit then level to see if you are tracking correctly. Always watch the yaw string to keep from slipping or skidding and do not look at the ground below. As the plane approaches the landing spot, the wind may become less enabling the plane to be swung slightly away from the wind during the descent. Just before touchdown, turn the plane to meet the on-rushing ground. This is sometimes called "kicking-out-the-crab." What you must do is to push hard on the rudder to align the wheels with the runway exactly at touchdown. In an ultralight without separate banking and rudder controls, it would be best to turn the whole plane into the wind just at touchdown and land across the runway at the last second. Learning to fly your ultralight in crosswinds without slipping or skidding is of utmost importance to competent airmanship.

How to Handle Wind Shear and Gusts

When flying in gusty air it is imperative that you be constantly aware of the airspeed. If the plane accelerates and the airspeed drops, continue the acceleration by quickly increasing the throttle and/or putting the nose down. When the plane decelerates with the airspeed increasing, slow the throttle and pitch the nose up. Handling gusts and wind shear is as simple as that, but to completely understand what's going on, let's look into the interesting mechanics of sudden changes in the wind.

Back in the "Golden Age" of aviation during the 1930's, along with the confusion about downwind turns, some pilots thought the inertia of the airplane was based on its ground speed. They said, for example, "A plane is on final at 35 mph with a headwind at 10 mph so its ground speed is 25 mph. If the wind stopped, the plane would be at 25 mph because its' inertia is still there based on its' ground speed." The pilot must add power and dive to regain the 35 mph flying speed. Or, "If you were going to parachute from an airplane going 150 mph, you would feel a wind of 150 mph the instant you stepped out, at least until drag slowed you down, because your inertia is based on the 150 mph ground speed." What they didn't consider was the situation in winds. Say our plane is going 35 mph in still air — the

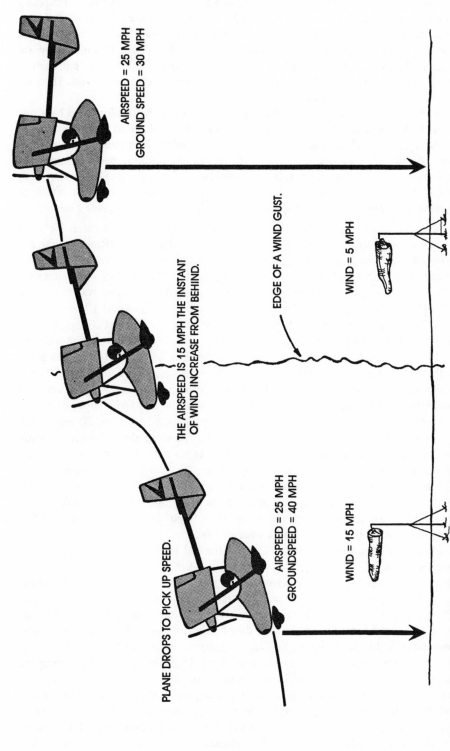

AIRSPEED = 25 MPH
GROUND SPEED = 30 MPH

EDGE OF A WIND GUST.

WIND = 5 MPH

THE AIRSPEED IS 15 MPH THE INSTANT
OF WIND INCREASE FROM BEHIND.

PLANE DROPS TO PICK UP SPEED.

AIRSPEED = 25 MPH
GROUNDSPEED = 40 MPH

WIND = 15 MPH

Fig. 2-17. This is what happens when a gust arises from behind.

45

ground speed is 35 mph. A gust of 10 mph from behind will instantaneously drop the airspeed to 25 mph! The ground speed is still 35 mph but that has no meaning at all because the plane in the air needs 35 mph to fly — the pilot must push the nose down and advance the throttle. The pilot must remember that both his and the inertia of his airplane is in reference only to the system in which they are immersed, which is the air. Only when the plane touches another system, such as the ground, is the aircraft's speed relative to the new system important. Here are but a few of the countless examples.

Perhaps you can have fun discussing these situations with pilots who have not thought about them. If a plane is going 50 mph into a 40 mph wind, the ground speed is 10 mph. If the plane hits something attached to the ground, such as a kite, tree, or hill, it will bump at 10 mph because its ground speed is important whenever the ground is touched. If the plane hits a balloon floating in the air, it will strike with its air inertia of 50 mph, since they're both in the same reference system. In the air, the ground speed has nothing to do with the plane's inertia!

To help understand systems, let's look at some everyday experiences. Picture a person running on one of the moving sidewalks at a big airport. Running with the sidewalk the speeds are added, but only in reference to something not on the treadmill. Likewise, when going against the treadmill the speed of the walkway is subtracted from your running speed. If you're going 10 mph on a walkway going 10 mph, you will bump someone standing still on the walkway at 10 mph. If you bumped into someone not on the walkway, the blow would be at 20 mph because that person is out of your system of reference. If you're going against the walkway at 11 mph, you would bump that same person at only 1 mph. If a person going with the walkway at 10 mph stepped off, the immediate speed would be 20 mph which might be dangerous to bystanders. But, if the person ran 20 mph against the walkway, only 10 mph would be the speed leaving the end and the person would have to push his legs hard and accelerate strongly to reach his 20 mph pace.

So what does all this mean to ultralights? Simply and emphatically this: **It must be understood that ground speed has nothing to do with the action of the plane in the air!** The plane is affected only by the air. It's as if the earth did not exist! The airspeed is the thing to watch because the pressure of the air on the wings and control surfaces tells you how to fly the plane for proper control. Watch the airspeed in windy air, stand up and shout it — fix it in your sub, semi and full consciousness. In a nutshell — **watch your airspeed!**

More examples. Say you're heading for the old landing patch and a gust hits you from behind, or a lull occurs from the wind in front, its all the same. Your airspeed is instantaneously less whatever the gust has subtracted from it. If you are going 30 mph, a rear gust of 15 mph makes the airspeed instantaneously 15 mph. The plane will stall and pitch down, assuming it's properly designed and balanced. Since the speed has been cut in half, drag has been reduced four times, so it will dive and pick up speed as well. You feel an acceleration and see the ground coming up. An inexperienced seat-of-the-pants pilot would probably pull the nose up as automatically as a reflex. The plane loses more airspeed and therefore, lift is even less. Now the ground is very close and our inexperienced pilot is too low off the end of the landing spot so, of course, he noses up even more. Smack! The plane is sitting in the bushes short of the landing spot. Even with last minute added power, the plane may still drop because it's in the nose-up, high drag attitude known as the

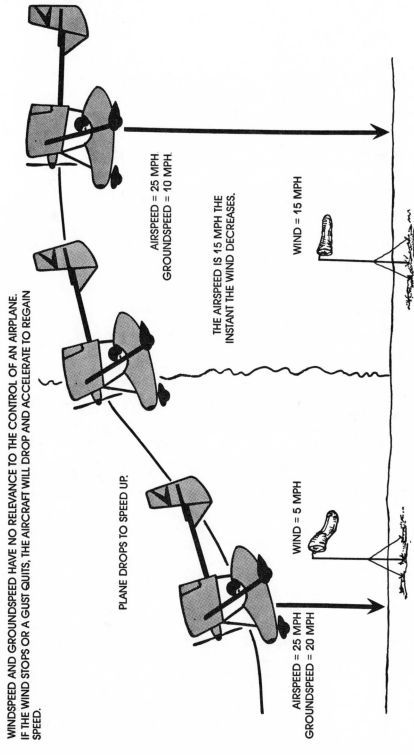

WINDSPEED AND GROUNDSPEED HAVE NO RELEVANCE TO THE CONTROL OF AN AIRPLANE. IF THE WIND STOPS OR A GUST QUITS, THE AIRCRAFT WILL DROP AND ACCELERATE TO REGAIN SPEED.

AIRSPEED = 25 MPH.
GROUNDSPEED = 10 MPH.

THE AIRSPEED IS 15 MPH THE INSTANT THE WIND DECREASES.

WIND = 15 MPH

PLANE DROPS TO SPEED UP.

WIND = 5 MPH

AIRSPEED = 25 MPH
GROUNDSPEED = 20 MPH

Fig. 2-18. If the wind stops or a gust quits, the aircraft will drop and accelerate to gain speed.

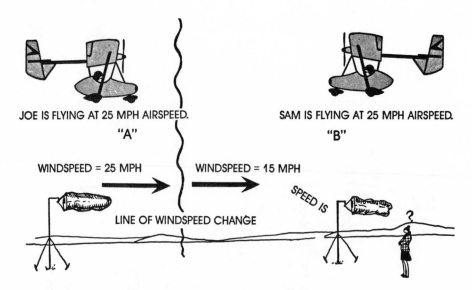

JOE IS FLYING AT 25 MPH AIRSPEED.

"A"

SAM IS FLYING AT 25 MPH AIRSPEED.

"B"

WINDSPEED = 25 MPH

WINDSPEED = 15 MPH

SPEED IS

LINE OF WINDSPEED CHANGE

Fig. 2-19. Testing your knowledge of airspeed and groundspeed.

JOE AND SAM ARE FLYING IDENTICAL ULTRALIGHTS AND BOTH PILOTS WEIGH 170 POUNDS·

1. JOE'S GROUNDSPEED AT "A" IS   ____
2. AT THE INSTANT OF WINDSPEED CHANGE, JOE'S   ____
3. AFTER FLYING IN THE 15 MPH TAILWIND, JOE'S GROUNDSPEED IS   ____
4. TO A PERSON ON THE GROUND, SAM WOULD SEEM TO BE GOING   ____
5. IF SAM AND JOE COLLIDE HEAD-ON, THEY WOULD STRIKE AT A SPEED OF   ____

ANSWERS
1. 50 MPH, BECAUSE GROUNDSPEED IS THE SUM OF AIRSPEED PLUS TAILWIND.
2. AT THAT INSTANT, THE AIRSPEED WOULD INCREASE TO 35 MPH. THE PLANE WOULD CLIMB AND DECELERATE BACK TO 25 MPH.
3.   GROUNDSPEED IS NOW 40 MPH BECAUSE THE TAILWIND OF 15 MPH ADDS TO THE 25 MPH AIRSPEED.
4. SAM WOULD SEEM TO BE GOING ONLY 10 MPH TO A GROUND OBSERVER. ALTHOUGH HIS AIRSPEED IS A STEADY 25 MPH, THE 15 MPH HEADWIND MAKES HIS SPEED OVER THE GROUND 10 MPH.
5. THE IMPACT VELOCITY WOULD BE EQUIVALENT TO 25 MPH! REMEMBER, FOR EVERY ACTION THERE IS AN EQUAL BUT OPPOSITE REACTION. ANOTHER WAY TO LOOK AT IT IS TO ASSUME THAT THE PLANE IS HITTING A BRICK WALL, PROVIDED BOTH AIRCRAFT ARE TRAVELLING AT THE SAME SPEED UPON IMPACT. THE RESULTS ARE IDENTICAL.

"backside-of-the-power-curve" (Here, there is simply more drag than the engine can overcome). Big jets are particularly susceptible to these wind shear gust incidences, because a jet engine takes six to eight seconds from throttle advance to the time it produces thrust. The big plane has its wheels and flaps down and will not accelerate quickly even when the power finally does come on.

In gusty weather, watch the airspeed and use your seat-of-the-pants feelings to react this way: (1) When you feel the plane accelerate, continue the acceleration by adding power or nosing down. It means a gust has come from behind or the wind has quit. If you looked at the airspeed, you would see it had dropped. (2) When you feel the plane suddenly slow and start to nose up it indicates a gust from the front, or the tail wind has stopped. To continue the path you wish, throttle back to let the plane slow down. The sensation of slowing means the plane has hit a gust from in front greatly raising its drag. The nose will try to pitch up and the airspeed will have increased.

Summary of Flying In The Wind

- In low turns, watch yaw and airspeed.
- Look at the ground for split seconds only.
- Climbing into a faster wind gradient adds performance.
- Obstacles slow the wind and drop your airspeed when flying upwind.
- Obstacles increase your airspeed when flying downwind.
- A crab is always straight and level but ground track is sideways.
- During takeoff and landing, crab into the wind.
- At touchdown or the beginning of takeoff, go straight on the ground, but in the air go straight into the wind.
- Airspeed is most important in gusts and shears.
- Continue accelerating in a lull, but slow down in a gust.
- Ignore ground speed!

Chapter Three~
Ultralights and
Thermals

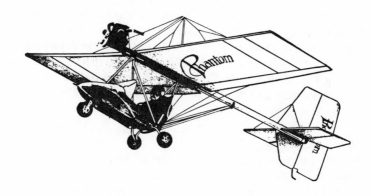

Ultralights and Thermals

Flying in thermal upcurrents is a fine way to get free horsepower and it makes ultralight flying immensely more fun. The engine can be stopped and flight continued with the quiet, rustling whistle of pure soaring while still gaining altitude. The skill and understanding required to soar successfully is a far more exciting challenge than jamming along with the howl of the engine and snarl of the propeller. To climb over mountains or high ground, soaring is almost indispensable. Knowing how to fly thermals will make you a safer pilot. You'll be able to leave those fearful morning and late afternoon flyers, with their fear of "bumps," in the dust! You'll out perform them and be capable of handling the machine in a wider range of situations.

What Makes A Thermal

A thermal rises because it is a mass of air lighter than the air surrounding it. It is lighter because it is less dense. But, how can one bunch of air be less dense than the rest you ask? Air is made up of a mechanical mixture of molecules of nitrogen, oxygen, and trace amounts of other elements like argon, neon, carbon dioxide, etc. It's held to the earth by gravity and it gets thinner with altitude. About half of all the air is in the first 18,000 feet. These air molecules bounce around against each other at a speed depending on their temperature.

The French scientist Charles found that the pressure of an enclosed volume of air increases with temperature, as the molecules push harder against the walls at a higher energy level. When air is heated outside of a container, its pressure cannot rise, since nothing is holding it in, therefore it expands. If a certain amount of air is spread over a larger space, it has less weight per cubic foot and is thus lighter than the same volume of unheated air.

Water vapor is also lighter than air, so the addition of evaporative moisture to a mass of air will also make it lighter. We think of water as a rather heavy liquid but if air were a liquid, it would be even heavier! When water becomes a vapor or a gas, it's much lighter than air.

So, if air is heated, humid, or both, it will rise through a cooler and/or drier air mass. The water in the thermal upcurrent often does another good thing for soaring pilots. The heat it took to evaporate the water is released when the vapor condenses back into liquid droplets to form a cloud. This adds heat to the air which can boost the upcurrents even more.

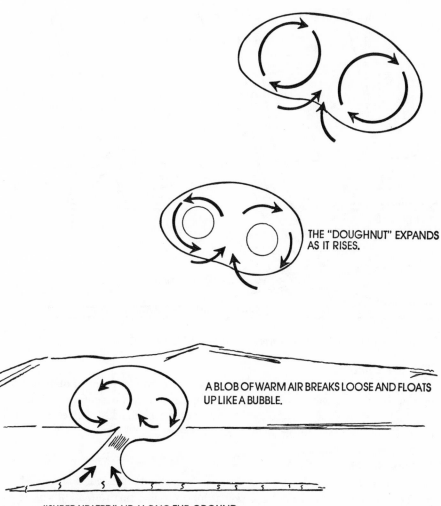

THE "DOUGHNUT" EXPANDS AS IT RISES.

A BLOB OF WARM AIR BREAKS LOOSE AND FLOATS UP LIKE A BUBBLE.

"SUPER HEATED" AIR ALONG THE GROUND.

Fig. 3-1. The "vortex ring thermal theory" is often mentioned in books and articles on soaring, but the "mysterious" ring has never been seen.

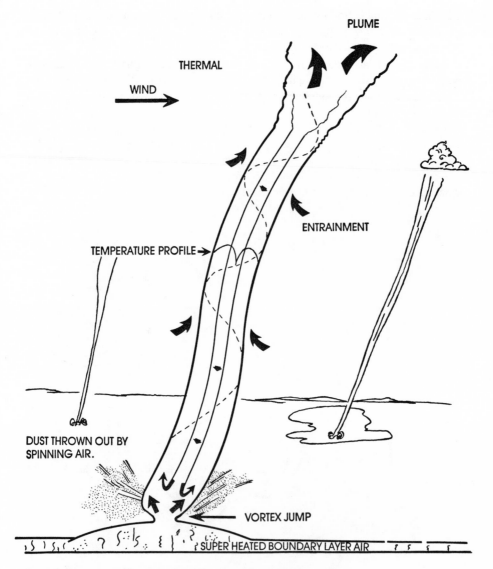

Fig. 3-2. The construction of a thermal. (Courtesy J. Mullen, USC.)

Thermal Shapes

What does a thermal look like? Thermals have been compared to bubbles rising in a pan of boiling water or to balloons of hot air. Since we cannot see a thermal, their actual shapes can only be guessed at by observing the dust they carry or their effects. There is disagreement about thermal shapes.

Vortex Bubbles

In England about 30 years ago, some experimenters released discrete blobs of powder into a glass sided pool and saw a doughnut-like ring formation sink to the bottom. Their tests looked similar to an upside down version of the whirling vortex mushroom clouds of an atomic bomb explosion. Thus, the vortex ring theory of thermals was born. A thermal was just like a smoke ring going up. Based on this analogy, thermals were described as a warm bubble that rose into the air in the form of a vortex ring, with the strongest upcurrent in the middle. Birds, they reasoned, could circle in this vortex ring bubble and continue climbing. Even though the bird is sinking relative to the upcurrent, the center of the thermal bubble is rising faster than the bird's sink rate, enabling it to sustain or climb.

Thermal Columns

While this is all very interesting and seems perfectly logical, the disagreement has risen because no one has ever seen such a vortex ring thermal. Many thousands of thermals have been and can be seen to be columns. Perhaps some thermals are bubbles and the vortex ring theory *may* be correct, but I have been soaring 35 years and have never seen one. The only ones ever observed are columns, some stretching over 8,000 feet high. Based on my experience and every glider pilot I know, the evidence for the vortex ring thermal is zilch.

Experiments using a hot plate in a specially constructed thermal making machine, have produced very consistent visualization of thermal column upcurrents as observed in nature. Since the evidence, both experimentally and in real life is so overwhelmingly in favor of thermal columns, I shall ignore the thermal "bubble" except as a figure of speech.

Birth of a Thermal Column

The sun heats the ground but does little heating of the air through which it has shined. This results in a layer of air warmed, not by the sun, but by the ground immediately below. This layer of hot air does not rise, even though it is lighter than the surrounding air — it tends to stick to the ground just like water to your hands. Eventually, the first foot above the ground becomes super heated. You can see this layer of air because it refracts light differently and often forms a mirage. You have seen that water-like shimmer when you approach the brow of a rise in the

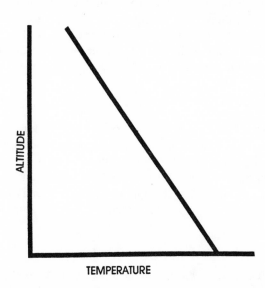

Fig. 3-3. A lapse rate conducive to good soaring occurs when the temperature decreases steadily with height.

55

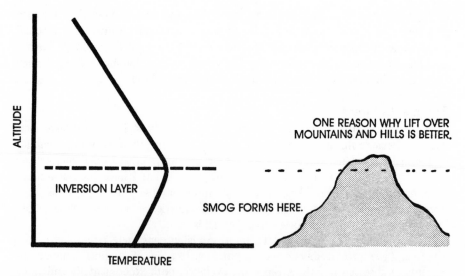

Fig. 3-4. When the temperature becomes warmer with height, an inversion is said to exist, and air will not rise because its buoyancy is dampened.

road and are looking through the super heated layer. It takes a disturbance to pull the hot air loose, perhaps a car passing or the gentle swirling of the wind blowing around an obstacle. Once the hot air has broken loose, it rises.

The air begins whirling as it rises and pulls together into a column. Spin on your heel with your arms outstretched, then pull your arms in and you will understand how the air gathering into a thermal column develops its whirl. The rotating air causes a lower pressure area in the center of the thermal, so it draws up all the hot air around it that has been sticking to the ground. Thus, it can feed itself as it moves and continues to rise into a tall column.

As it rises, air is pulled in which cools the thermal, and since the air becomes less dense with altitude, the thermal expands. Expansion results in cooling. Eventually, the tightly spinning upcurrent spreads into a plume, similar to smoke rising from a chimney, and slows. In the strongest thermals, the core is a down draft. How far a thermal will rise, as well as its strength, is determined by the lapse rate.

Lapse Rate

The lapse rate is the change in temperature with altitude. If the air is cooler, say five to seven degrees fahrenheit for each thousand feet, the thermal will continue rising rapidly, even though its heat is diminishing as it expands. Remember, it is the difference in temperature between the thermal and the surrounding air that makes one air mass lighter than another. I have seen 115 degree days in the desert with no thermals, while experiencing powerful thermals in cool, cloudy weather.

Inversions

An inversion occurs when air temperature increases with altitude. The Los Angeles Basin is a good example of an inversion caused by cool sea air trapped underneath the hot air from the desert. The hot exhaust from steam plants,

56

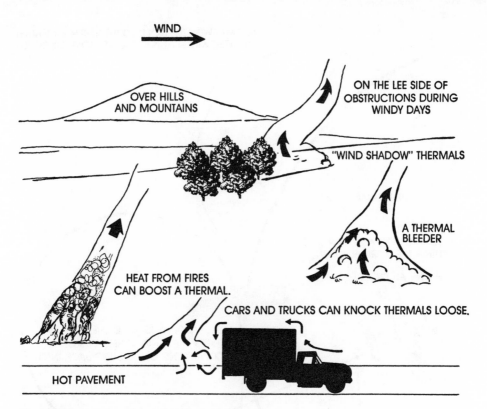

WIND →

OVER HILLS
AND MOUNTAINS

ON THE LEE SIDE OF
OBSTRUCTIONS DURING
WINDY DAYS

"WIND SHADOW" THERMALS

A THERMAL
BLEEDER

HEAT FROM FIRES
CAN BOOST A THERMAL.

CARS AND TRUCKS CAN KNOCK THERMALS LOOSE.

HOT PAVEMENT

Fig. 3-5. Where thermals are likely to be found.

industry, and motor vehicles rises very nicely until it reaches the inversion. By then it has cooled, so its temperature is no different from the air above, and it stops rising. Eventually, it will fill the volume below the inversion with smelly fumes.

You can see an inversion almost anywhere in the country just after sunrise, when the air nearest the surface of the earth has cooled over night. Notice the smoke layering at 100 feet or less and fog forming in the coolest places? You can often feel the sudden difference in temperature when flying open cockpit and break through the inversion.

Where to Find Thermals — Unstable Weather Lift

Thermals can be found on cloudy days and over water. Sunshine is not necessary if a cold air mass moves over a warmer surface. Water holds heat well and cold air moving over a lake or ocean can result in thermals. Gulls often make use of such lift. The clouds of stormy weather, harbor good upcurrents below their unstable innards.

Sun Thermals

In general, most thermals we use will be on pleasant, sunny days. You can even predict when the following day will have good soaring by looking at the night sky. If the stars twinkle a lot, it shows the air is unstable. When the stars are steady, the next day will be calm with less lift.

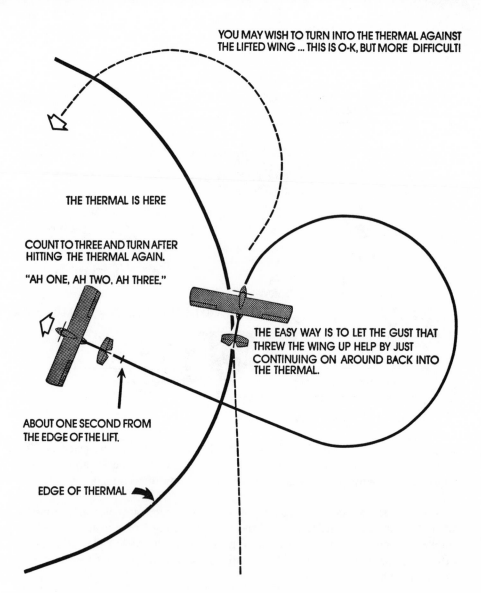

Fig. 3-6. How to enter a thermal.

Thermal Bleeders and Shakers

The obvious place to find thermals is over the hottest bits of ground such as roads, parking lots, bare fields or factory rooftops. Places to find "bleeders" include, over a hill, isolated rocks, or hummocks because the heated air will flow up the sides and bleed off the top. The more isolated the "thermal bleeder" the more certain you will find an upcurrent over it. I have also found roads excellent thermal makers because the cars rush by shaking the hot air loose.

Wind Shadow Thermals

On windy days, thermals form behind obstructions because the wind doesn't blow away the warmed air, while mixing it up. The air can sit long enough to warm up into a nice mass before it begins its whirling ascent. These are called "wind shadow" thermals.

Heat and Fire Thermals

Burning fields or bonfires make fine lift if not too large, provided the lapse rate is good enough to accelerate the hot air from the fire. If the smoke flattens, it is a good sign of an inversion and poor upcurrents.

Don't try to fly over a big fire. I tried soaring over a forest fire at Elsinore and it felt like I was in a jeep going 60 mph over a rocky creekbed.

Some think ultralights are too dangerous to fly in thermals, yet hang gliders, from which ultralights were developed, thermal perfectly well, and this is the main joy of their pilots. If an ultralight is not controllable or strong enough to take a few bumps, good heavens, don't even fly it in calm air. You never know when gusty winds will arise.

How to Fly Thermals

There's no reason why a properly designed ultralight cannot climb in thermals or even strong dust devils, just as safely as any glider. But, you ask, exactly how do you climb thermals?

Thermal soaring takes practice and understanding. The unending interest of thermaling is that you can never do it perfectly. Trying to fly at the speed for lowest sink and the best circle to stay in the lift is a great challenge.

When I was a student at the University of Illinois, we had a little open cockpit glider. We towed it with a Ford hot rod tied to a thousand feet of wire. I had read every book about centering the lift and gaining altitude in those mysterious and invisible columns of air. In over 250 flights I climbed high above the bellowing open pipe V-8, released and began a quiet glide from 800 feet always searching for a thermal. When I found lift I followed the experts' advice. "Count three, then turn. Bank steep when in the strongest lift and flatten out in the poor lift." Maneuvering the little glider, altering the bank, and counting I consistently managed to lose the lift. After graduation, I took a ride in a two-seater with an experienced thermal flier and quickly discovered my problem. In many years of instructing student glider pilots about soaring, I have often explained what I learned in that one flight years ago. It is this: fly around in smooth circles as slowly and roundly as possible and quit working so hard to "center" the thermal. Those of us who fly towline gliders have found how often they will stay up if the model is set for a circle after release. If there are any thermals at all, the model will usually stay up. It's the same for ultralights.

When beginning to learn soaring, a simple smooth turn is as good a way to fly a thermal as any. Say you are flying over a likely thermal producer, such as a parking lot or raised ground and feel a bump, shove, or lift, as the plane flies into an upcurrent. Turn in either direction. I always turn the way the thermal tilts the plane. Some say this will carry you away from the thermal, but I have found just the opposite. Why? Provided you quickly and positively continue the turn already begun by the natural bank imparted by the lift, the plane makes an immediate circle directly back into the lift!

Most important is to keep the circle round, by a steady angle of bank and constant speed. At this stage of learning, don't worry about finding the best part of his lift, that will come later. Round circles, without diving, skidding, or skipping, are more important. Thermals are bouncy so it takes skilled maneuvering to keep the ship going around evenly. The speed should be slow because, in almost all ultralights, this results in the lowest sink. The throttle should be set to fly the plane level. Learning is faster with the engine on because there's less chance of falling out of the lift. As you climb in the thermal, by making gentle circles, you may notice the plane seems to be rising more in some part of the turn. Don't worry about this but concentrate on perfect circles. To keep from skidding or slipping, look at the horizon, not at the ground sliding around at the wing tip. The horizon should "move" smoothly by at the same speed, without the plane changing pitch. — Your rate of turn should be constant.

Thermal Practice

Your first thermal practicing might be in the early morning to 10:30 a.m. or after 5 p.m. when the thermals are weakly beginning or quietly dying. At first, you might try slowing down and flying straight ahead through the thermal. Nose down and keep going until you run into another thermal, when again you should slow down to stay in the lift. This "porpoising" can increase your climb and be a good introduction to sensing upcurrents. When you feel more confident in these slightly bumpy conditions, you can venture further into mid-day when the lift is stronger and likely to be more turbulent.

Sensing Lift

There are many ways to tell if you are in a thermal without using specialized instruments. The airspeed will increase when encountering lift due to the natural stability of the airplane. The angle of attack increases when moving into the

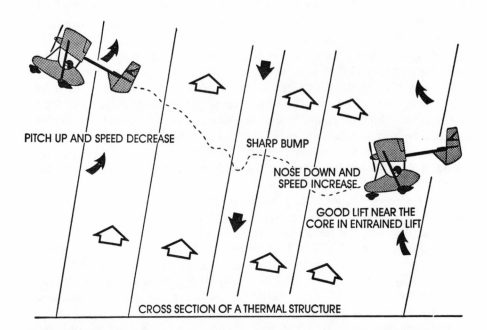

PITCH UP AND SPEED DECREASE

SHARP BUMP

NOSE DOWN AND SPEED INCREASE

GOOD LIFT NEAR THE CORE IN ENTRAINED LIFT

CROSS SECTION OF A THERMAL STRUCTURE

Fig. 3-7. Prepare for several changes in pitch and airspeed while crossing a thermal

upcurrent. If you pulled up in a climb and let go of the controls, a good ultralight will nose down to its trimmed speed automatically. When flying into lift, it will also try to stabilize and, in so doing, will pick up speed. Feeling the surge of lift and watching the airspeed increase is one way to know you have gone into an upcurrent. Down low, watching the ground move away, and being able to see farther, is an effective way to tell if you are climbing. But, for learning to work upcurrents best, you need a variometer.

The Variometer

By circling after feeling the lift, good climbing can be accomplished, but this has limitations because humans are unable to sense altitude differences. If the plane is flying in a downdraft and goes into smooth air, it feels like "lift" and you are fooled into thinking you're going up.

A special, very sensitive rate of climb instrument, called a variometer, has been developed that will register changes in altitude very quickly. Let's discuss the various types!

Pithball Type

They all use a tank, which is usually a thermos bottle (to minimize temperature effects on air volume), connected by a T fitting to small tubes. One line of the T goes to the bottom of a tapering hole in a plastic block. The other is fitted to the top of a second tapering hole. Inside these holes are lightweight balls. If the plane rises into less dense air, the flow out of the bottle due to the lower pressure pushes the small ball up out of the bottom of its tapering hole. Since this ball is is usually green the pilot knows he is rising and often refers to upcurrents as "green air." When the plane sinks, the air is pushed into the thermos bottle from the open bottom of the other tapering tube which has a red ball in it. The tubes are tapered so the rate of flow can be measured by the height of the little balls in

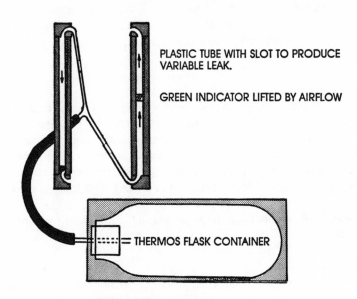

PLASTIC TUBE WITH SLOT TO PRODUCE VARIABLE LEAK.

GREEN INDICATOR LIFTED BY AIRFLOW

THERMOS FLASK CONTAINER

Fig. 3-8. The pellet, or pith ball type, variometer.

61

the tubes. The higher the little ball is lifted, the more air is flowing past it, and, therefore, the rate of climb or sink can be seen. Cost is around $50.

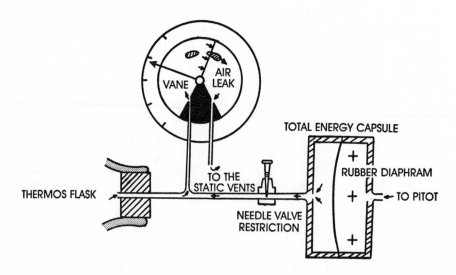

Fig. 3-9. The mechanical, or vane type, variometer.

Mechanical Type

A mechanical variometer, at $190, is a regular aircraft instrument with a pointer to show the rate of climb. It has an internal chamber with a carefully fitted vane on fine bearings, with a hairspring to keep the needle centered. Air flowing in or out of the instrument pushes the vane, thus moving the needle on the face of the vario-meter. Calibrated slots allow the air to escape at a rate depending on the position of the vane, thus indicating how fast the altitude change is taking place. This may sound crude, but careful design and precision manufacture have made them very smooth and reliable.

Electric

At $200 or more, the electronic variometer is even more reliable as far as vibration and bumps are concerned. An electric current heats a thermister, a device which changes its resistance depending on temperature. One thermister is in the out channel and one in the in channel of the thermos bottle. The minute air flow slightly cools the thermister, thus dropping its resistance which can be amplified and shown on a sensitive electric meter. This changing electric signal can be used to modify a tone through either earphones or a loudspeaker so the pilot does not have to look at the dial but can keep his eyes outside, looking for signs of lift and other aircraft.

Total Energy

Some variometers have "total energy" compensation, which is not so critical in ultralights because of the small speed range and high drag. Nevertheless, you can make a variometer read "climb" if you nose up and turn your speed into height.

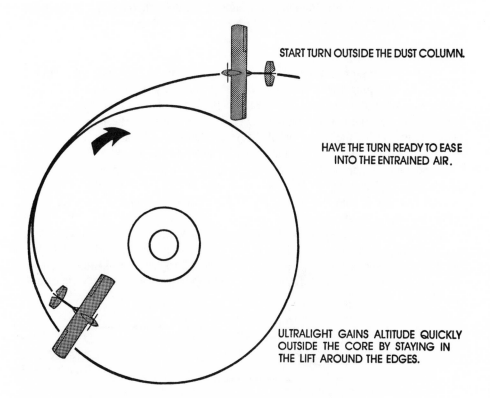

START TURN OUTSIDE THE DUST COLUMN.

HAVE THE TURN READY TO EASE INTO THE ENTRAINED AIR.

ULTRALIGHT GAINS ALTITUDE QUICKLY OUTSIDE THE CORE BY STAYING IN THE LIFT AROUND THE EDGES.

Fig. 3-10. How to tie into a dust devil.

This is called a "stick thermal" because it is the result of trading speed for climb, which soon dissipates while the "climb" drops quickly. A total energy device added to a variometer puts the airspeed into consideration so, if the speed decreases, the needle shows less "up" than it would in a straight pull up. The simplest is a small plastic can divided by a diaphragm. The airspeed is connected to the diaphragm which flexes, depending upon the airspeed and modifies the variometer accordingly. The advantage is, that it tells the pilot when the airplane is going up because of atmospheric lift instead of turning speed into climb. Some pilots are very sensitive to acceleration and climb and can mentally compensate to eliminate the confusion of "stick thermals."

Thermal Sniffing

With a good variometer and the ability to maneuver the ultralight with ease and precision, you can begin more efficient thermal techniques. Watch the variometer and look out at the scenery to relate the strongest part of the lift with a check point. After a few circles, to make sure the point of best lift has not changed, correct your turn to head in that direction. Make only about a three second direction change then roll smoothly back into exactly the same radius turn as before. By continually edging into the good lift, you will have a steady climb all the way around.

If you keep falling out of the same side of the thermal, no matter how many times you keep straightening out and heading into the lift, try this: at the point of maximum lift, quickly reverse your turn to circle the other way.

Review of Turning

Stalling is common in thermal soaring, since the turn is slow and tight. Do not recover by stopping the turn and diving. Instead, stay at the same bank angle but briefly pitch down a little bit to reduce the angle of attack, and keep right on circling. Because the lower wing is going so much slower than the upper or outside wing, its lift is much less. For ultralights with ailerons this means the inside aileron is held down or "out" of the turn and the rudder held "into" the turn. These "crossed-controls" are to keep a coordinated, no skidding or slipping, turn at very slow speed. If the inside wing starts to stall and drop, it can't be raised with more aileron. At speeds near the stall, applying down aileron to pick up a wing won't cause that wing to stall. What does happen is greatly increased drag which yaws that wing back, increasing its angle of attack, aggravating the stall. If you wish to pick up the wing at slow speed, stop the yaw by using lots of rudder. If it does stall, don't do anything except pitch the nose down slightly by releasing the back pressure on the stick or shifting your weight slightly forward on weight shift ultralights.

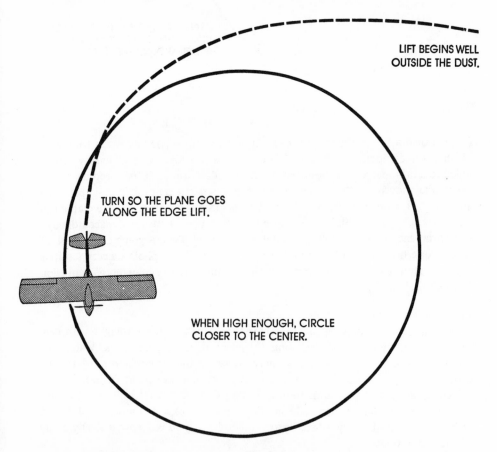

Fig. 3-11. Edging into a dust column for safest climb.

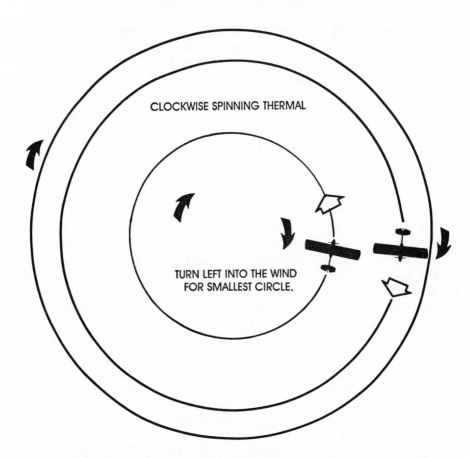

CLOCKWISE SPINNING THERMAL

TURN LEFT INTO THE WIND
FOR SMALLEST CIRCLE.

IN THEORY, THERMALS SHOULD TURN CLOCKWISE IN THE NORTHERN HEMISPHERE, BUT IN PRACTICE, THEY TURN EITHER WAY. SO WATCH THE DUST IF POSSIBLE. IF NOT, TURN LEFT.

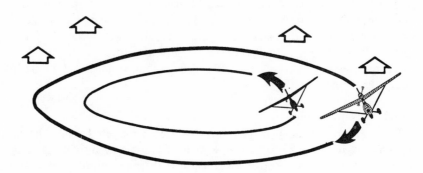

BOTH PLANES HAVE THE SAME SPEED AND BANK ANGLE AND MAKE A CIRCLE IN THE SAME TIME, BUT THE PLANE GOING TOWARD THE WIND MAKES A SMALLER CIRCLE AND SHOULD THEREFORE BE IN THE STRONGER LIFT.

Fig. 3-12. Which way should you turn in a thermal?

65

Eventually, you'll reach the altitude you wish or the thermal weakens, which always gives rise to the question: have I fallen out the side, or has the lift weakened? Only trial and error, experience with other thermals the same day, or by looking at the other airplanes soaring with you, can answer that question. If a few sorties out and around the thermal find not much better lift, you may as well fire up the engine and go on or just advance the throttle if you're idling. Thermal flying is like skiing or surfing. You can never do it perfectly, but flying slow in steep banks is the finest practice for the feel of stall and subtle recovery so important for safety.

Flying in Dust Devils

If you're looking for a thermal and you see a whopping big dust devil ahead, should you try to climb in it? Of course. Sailplanes have been doing it for decades, but it does take a pilot with understanding and practice. Start by entering at about 2000 feet high, where the lift is wider. Instead of flying directly into the center, aim at the edge and have the ship ready in a turn designed to circle about 25 yards outside. If you fly straight in, the sharp lift at the edges and down air in the center throws you around so much, it is impossible to establish a good circle.

After you have practiced going around the dust devil and gained more height in its wonderfully strong upcurrents, tighten the circle and you'll go up like "tissue-paper-up-the-chimney!" The higher you enter, the smoother the lift — the whirling action at the center is less when it spreads out into a rising plume.

Low altitudes in dust devils are more difficult. The bank of lift outside the dust is much narrower near the ground so the ship must be brought in closer to the turbulent center. Again, head for the edge with your turn already started. Do not go directly in, unless you have a lot of experience doing this in sailplanes. I have used whopping big thermals for "saves" on cross country glider flights and found that the turbulence and gusts can stall the ship suddenly. If close to the ground, say 400 to 700 feet, there is certainly room for a sharp pilot to recover, but for a novice, this is too low and he must land immediately. An ultralight with power on is not in quite such a serious predicament, but its slow speed means it will be tossed around more. The lift will be strong enough to raise you quickly. When you are established in a climb and have gained more altitude, gradually edge your circles closer. It will be turbulent and yield strong lift but hardly unconquerable.

Which Way to Circle

Some experts recommend you always circle to the left because thermals are supposed to swirl clockwise in the Northern Hemisphere. By circling against the wind the G loading is supposedly less because the plane is not circling with such a high ground speed. With the G loading less, the sink would therefore be less — partly. Having looked down at many thermals, I notice they turn in either direction. At 35 mph in a 30 degree bank, your G loading will be the same whether you are turning with the wind or against the wind.

Although your G loading will be the same and the circle will be completed in exactly the same time, there will be a difference in the radius of the turn! In actual flight we don't notice a change in radius because there is no marker in the middle of the thermal. The closer you can circle to the center of the thermal, presumably, the stronger lift; therefore, in the Northern Hemisphere circle left unless you definitely see the thermal spinning counter clockwise.

Summary of Ultralights and Thermals

- Hot and/or humid air will rise in a cooler air mass.
- Thermals are a whirling column of rising air.
- Air, cooling rapidly with height, is good for lift.
- An inversion blocks lift and occurs in early morning and evening.
- Thermals are found where they have some way to break loose — hills, turbulence, or above roads.
- Slow down in upcurrents, and speed up through downcurrents.
- Round circles are most important to soaring. Watch your airspeed, and the yaw string.
- Use a variometer to make slight adjustments into the strongest lift.
- Fly into dust devils at a tangent.
- Tight turns on the stall mean quick changes in your angle of attack, to stay in the turn at minimum sink.
- Circle into the whirl to make a smaller radius.

"Watch Your Airspeed."

Chapter Four~ Ultralights and Slope Soaring

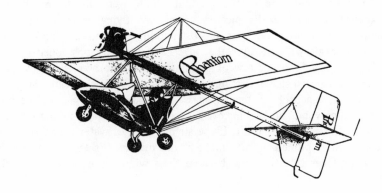

Ultralights and Slope Soaring

The most direct use of the wind, to climb over hills and mountains and to inexpensively practice the niceties of perfect flying, is by using the updrafts created when winds blow over an obstruction. You can stay up with the engine off because air will rise over the edge of a properly positioned mountain, sea cliff, or even a forest or row of buildings. When the wind flows over this slope, whatever its actual shape, it is pushed upwards to a much greater height than the obstruction, especially if the air mass is unstable. Warm air will be accelerated by the slope wind and become even more buoyant as it is pushed into the cooler air above, making for fine lift. If the air has a lot of water vapor, the cooling that occurs as it is pushed up may make clouds or rain. It's easy to see which side of any slope faces into the wind because there will be more and greener plants and trees.

Positioning

Let's assume a hill, perhaps 500 feet high, smooth, with no turbulence producing obstructions, and a landing ground at its base. The hill should face into the wind and be a mile long. We'll use this as a good example to explain the basics of slope soaring.

Take off into the wind near the hill's base. At 250 feet above the ground bank toward the hill so as to approach at a gentle angle. As the ultralight nears the face of the hill, turn to fly parallel with the top about 100 feet upwind. The

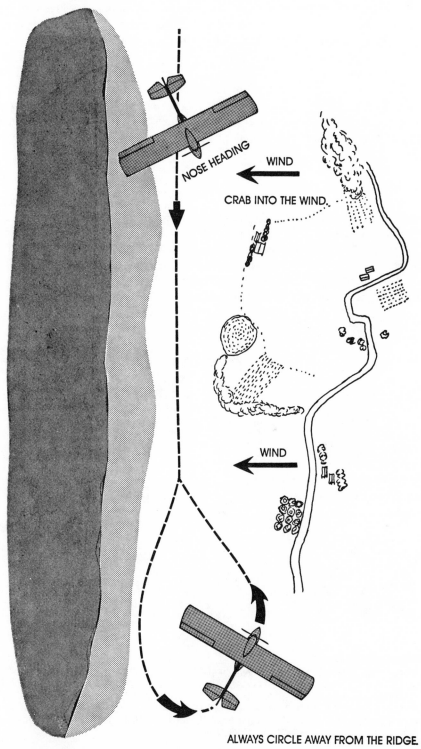

NOSE HEADING

WIND

CRAB INTO THE WIND.

WIND

ALWAYS CIRCLE AWAY FROM THE RIDGE.

Fig. 4-1. The "beat" as used in ridge soaring.

lift added to your climb will boost you to some point above the top, depending on the strength of the breeze and the lapse rate. A smooth sea breeze sweeping in from the ocean can create lift a few hundred feet above the top of the ridge. Then fly back and forth in front of the hill and stay up as long as you wish.

The most important practice is in keeping the yaw string centered, while positioned in front of the hill. This is known as crabbing. If the plane drifts back over the top of the hill, it could be blown into the down currents on the lee side. Too far ahead of the ridge and the lift will be very weak or disappear. It sounds simple, but it takes a good deal of airmanship and practice to keep an ultralight at just the right position, without slipping or skidding, To slope soar, you must crab.

Slipping

A common error is to put the upwind wing down and slip to stay in position in front of the slope. Slipping results in higher drag, since the plane is going sideways. If the lift is weak, the plane will not be able to stay up without adding power. The pilot may be confused by the slope of the ground. There is also a tendency to try to make the wings level in reference to the side of the hill instead of the true horizon. The other problem is the sideways movement of the ground. It seems more natural to point the nose in the direction you want to go. But, to

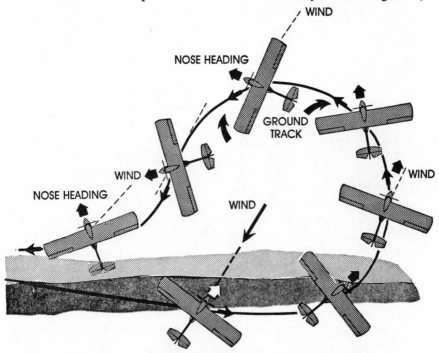

GREAT CARE AND AN UNDERSTANDING OF THE RELATIONSHIP BETWEEN THE WIND AND YOUR HEADING IS NECESSARY TO MAKE PROPER TURNS IN WIND STRONG ENOUGH TO ACCOMPLISH SOARING. AN UNTHINKING TURN WILL EASILY CARRY THE PLANE DIRECTLY INTO THE RIDGE OR BEHIND IT OR, AT THE LEAST, REQUIRE SOME STEEP AND RADICAL TURNS TO GET LINED UP AGAIN FOR THE BEAT BACK ALONG THE RIDGE. AGAIN, MUCH OF THE CONFUSION GETS BLAMED ON THE "WIND GRADIENT", WHICH IS NONSENSE.

Fig. 4-2. Making the turn at the upwind end of a ridge

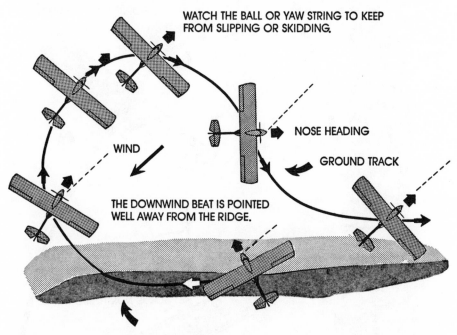

WATCH THE BALL OR YAW STRING TO KEEP
FROM SLIPPING OR SKIDDING.

NOSE HEADING

WIND

GROUND TRACK

THE DOWNWIND BEAT IS POINTED
WELL AWAY FROM THE RIDGE.

Fig. 4-3. The Turn at the downwind end of the ridge is very different from the upwind turn.

keep the nose straight and not be pushed into the hill, the windward wing must be tilted down so the aircraft slips into the wind.

Skidding

A less common mistake is to point too directly into the wind so the plane does not move along the slope. The pilot keeps the wings level but skids along sideways to keep in position, close to the hill. It takes concentration to keep the yaw string or ball centered, especially if the wind is gusty. Keep the yaw string straight and look out ahead to check wing level position with the horizon while watching your drift out of the corners of your eyes. If you look down at the hill, it will be confusing because the nose is pointing one way and the plane is crabbing along in a different direction. Instead of looking over the nose you will be looking out to the side toward the end of the ridge. After you become more experienced, you can look around and down without going into a slip or skid as easily as you did when you began.

The Beat

When the end of the ridge approaches, always turn away from the hill, and fly back remembering to compensate for the wind in the opposite direction. If the turn is made toward the hill, the plane can be blown over the top or into the side if you're too low.

The up and back pattern is repeated as long as you wish. It is fun to turn off the motor to see if the plane will stay up, and to fly at various speeds to discover the speed for lowest sink rate. You can also practice aerial restarts for confidence building.

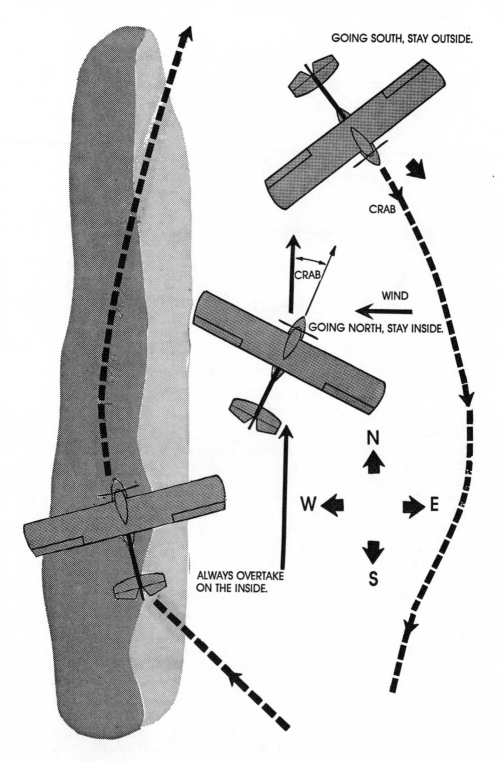

GOING SOUTH, STAY OUTSIDE.

CRAB

CRAB

WIND

GOING NORTH, STAY INSIDE.

N

W ← → E

S

ALWAYS OVERTAKE
ON THE INSIDE.

Fig. 4-4. The traffic rules of the ridge.

74

That's the basic idea for slope soaring and it's about as easy and relaxing a way to soar as possible. You can stay up as long as the wind blows into the ridge. On the windward side of Ohau in Hawaii, gliders have stayed up more than four days — about as close to glorified flag pole sitting as one can get.

Ridge Traffic

Often there are other aircraft using the same slope soaring site presenting the danger of a collision. It is fun to group together so you can keep a constant watch on your mates and, it's enjoyable to compare performance. By going in the same direction, there's less possibility of a catastrophic head-on collision.

Most ridges are aligned generally north and south. This is because the earth has separated into giant continental plates. Mountains rise where the plates are shoving against or diving below one another. Most of this action is in an east/west direction, so we have mountains north and south. The rule, therefore, is: aircraft flying northerly keep to the inside of the ridge and those going southerly stay on the outside track. If lift is very weak and you are going south, you can pull outside if you meet another plane and move back close to the ridge as soon as the conflict is passed, so you don't lose out on the stronger lift. If you are overtaking another ultralight, you should pass between that aircraft and the hill, no matter which direction you're going.

Overtake Inside

The usual rules of the air say the overtaker always stays to the right; but in the case of slope soaring in a southerly direction, you would be forced to pass another plane on the outside. Since turns are always made away from the ridge, an overtaken aircraft could unexpectedly turn into you. Therefore, when slope soaring, no matter what the rules of the air say, always overtake between the aircraft and the ridge to lessen the danger of a conflict if the other ship turns.

Wind at an Angle

If the wind is not directly into the hill, the pilot must modify his crab angle depending on whether the track, or "beat" (as slope soarers call it), is upwind or downwind. The nose must be pointed more away from the ridge when going downwind and, of course, less on the upwind beat. That's fairly simple to understand. More difficult, are the turns at the end of the beat. The turn at the end of the downwind run must be banked very steeply or it will be far wider than you expected. The turn at the end of the upwind beat will be so fast that, even with a moderate bank, you must be careful not to overdo it or you'll find yourself being whipped straight back into the ridge!

Steep Cliffs

Every slope soaring site does not have the perfect shape used to explain the basics of maneuvering along a ridge. If the slope is very steep, with a marked cut-off at the top (such as is found at Torrey Pines in California), it is important to know that the wind does not stay smooth over the top. Instead it bursts into eddies, with backward flow in some places and calm in others. Use was made of this fact at one of the Torrey Pines Glider Meets, in which was flying a 1-26 I had built. We bedded down with our sleeping bags and tent at the brow of the cliff. Some of our friends laughed at us. We were in calm air, while they struggled all night further back from the edge with the wind gusting and flapping their tent back and forth.

A very steep cliff has an area of turbulence or calm near its base also. Air can't follow the abrupt bottom corner and a backflow may develop. Many times at Torrey Pines, which has a perfect example of this condition, an ultralight glider will not stay up if it has dropped more than a quarter of the way from the top of the cliff! This is particularly true in a crosswind, where the lift will be gone below the sharp edge of the cliff. It does however, make for easy landings on the beach because it seems to eliminate what would ordinarily be a crosswind and replaces it with a calm.

I won a Torrey Pines Mid-Winter Championship by using this knowledge. Over 30 contestants were soaring back and forth over the cliff when a large rainstorm moved in from the Pacific. All but the top five contenders landed in the rain. After the storm passed, the wind began to shift to the south. The lift became less and less until it was limited to a few parts of the cliff that were at top end of small gullies. The one most likely to stay facing the wind longest was selected and tenaciously beat back and forth while making figure eights. One by one the competitors slipped slightly below the edge of the precipice and were soon on the beach. I was practically brushing the weeds with my wheel as I twisted and turned keeping position over that scrap of the cliff until I too, found myself even with the edge. The lift was immediately no more and I glided to the beach. But I was triumphant! My glider had stayed up over five hours which was a few minutes longer than anyone else. Hooray!

Lee Side Conditions

The greatest danger in flying, however, is getting behind that edge in the turbulent section. The pilot may have gone too far behind and makes a dive for the windward edge trying to get out into the upcurrents. Just when it looks as if the plane is going to make it, the reverse curl behind the edge may stall the wing, dropping it heavily. The danger of stalling onto the lee of the ridge is very great. Don't allow yourself to drift back too far, or approach a cliff from the downwind side close to the top. Just what is "too close" to the lee side of a ridge? That depends on many things: the shape of the hill, the speed of the wind, and the speed of the airplane. A faster plane can zip through the down air more quickly. If the wind is rather gentle and the air unstable, with a good lapse rate, the lift will be so good that air may be rising all around the top of the cliff and even be rising on the lee side. In that case, you have no problem crossing or getting into the lee of any ridge. A strong wind combined with stable air will result in great downdrafts hundreds of yards to the lee of the ridge. So now what do you do?

Crossing Ridges

Always approach any ridge at an angle, never straight on! If you find the downdraft nonexistent or rather slight, you can pass right over the ridge. If the sink is very strong, you can escape with a very slight turn and go off quickly beyond the area of sink. You can then come back higher to allow more space to dive through the sink. Most dangerous, is trying to follow a gulley up the center

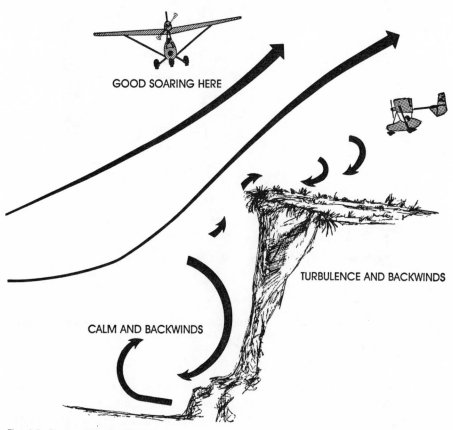

GOOD SOARING HERE

TURBULENCE AND BACKWINDS

CALM AND BACKWINDS

Fig. 4-5. Steep cliff conditions.

with little space to retrace your path. Downcurrents will often flood down a lee gulley far stronger than in any other place. On the upwind side, a gulley or canyon should be flown along its edge. Try to pick the side you think is most nearly windward to use whatever lift is available. Even if there is no lift, you have room to turn back in case of downcurrents. The wind aloft may have shifted and what you thought was the windward side may turn out to have downcurrents. Therefore, in approaching a ridge, always go at an angle and be ready to turn back if too low, or speed through if high enough.

Gullies

Hills commonly have erosion cut gullies and small canyons in their sides. Sometimes a ridge will be eroded into a large semicircle. This shape is the very best for soaring because the air is concentrated and the upcurrent increased. A bowl will also have updrafts over a wider range of wind directions because there is always some part of it that is directly into the wind. It will, of course, have a lee side in the case of a crosswind, even though there will be good lift over part of the bowl.

More common, is a serrated ridge with little gullies and canyons leading down the sides. This presents interesting problems for the slope soarer because there are so many lee edges. If the wind is straight on and you are flying along the top of the ridge, it is best to turn outward to stay in the apex of the gulley where the lift

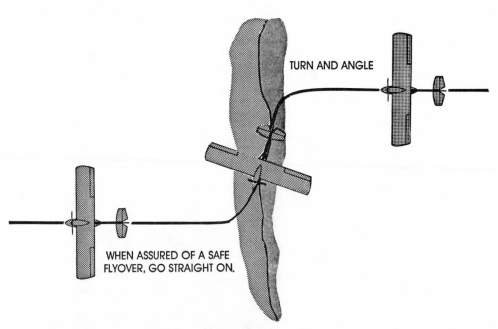

TURN AND ANGLE

WHEN ASSURED OF A SAFE
FLYOVER, GO STRAIGHT ON.

WHEN APPROACHING A RIDGE, ALWAYS CROSS AT AN ANGLE UNTIL YOU ARE SURE THERE ARE NOT HIDDEN DOWNCURRENTS, AND THAT YOU ARE HIGH ENOUGH.

Fig. 4-6. How to cross a ridge.

will be concentrated. If the wind is across, the upcurrents will be concentrated on the parts facing the wind, with turbulence and downdrafts in between.

During a five-hour flight over the Elsinore Mountains, I left the smooth lift near Inspiration Point and flew toward Mt. Pinos ("Saddleback") to see if I could get more lift over this higher section. Unfortunately, northwest of the lake it is so chopped up with ridges and gullies that the lift is not smooth. I soared along the face of a windward ridge climbing nicely until near the top of the canyon. Here the gullies come together and the upcurrent on one side met with the downcurrent from the other edge. My glider rolled and dropped into the gulley as if the wings had fallen off. I had a scare and decided to try again to see how to best fly this condition.

I have found that the safest way to fly ridges in a crosswind is to climb on the windward side until about a third of the way to the top, where the ridges start becoming quite narrow, then turn back out and fly into the wind until the lift from the windward ridge decreases. Now, turn and fly to the next ridge. Move back in and climb again until near the top, and turn away into the wind until lift decreases, and so on. The downcurrents are no stronger than the upcurrents so you can tell how far you must be from the cliff by noting where the lift drops off on the windward edge. The downcurrents on a lee ridge will be about the same distance. Eventually, if conditions are good, you will reach the top of the ridge where turbulence from the gullies and canyons will not be very bad, if at all.

Thermaling from the Ridge

If you are flying and hit a nice surge of extra lift, there's a great temptation to

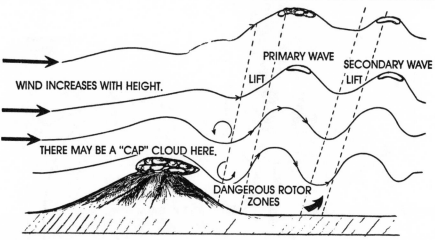

THERE MAY BE LENS SHAPED CLOUDS HERE.

PRIMARY WAVE

SECONDARY WAVE

WIND INCREASES WITH HEIGHT.

LIFT

LIFT

THERE MAY BE A "CAP" CLOUD HERE.

DANGEROUS ROTOR ZONES

Fig. 4-7. Cross section of a mountain wave.

circle. This can be dangerous because the wind may blow the ship back into the cliff during the downwind part of the turn.

I have made circles near Torrey Pines cliff. On the downwind part of the turn with the wind behind, it seemed certain I was going to smash against the face of the cliff. The temptation to tighten the turn is almost overwhelming, but the result would be a stall out of the turn, a spin, or quick mush into the cliff with the wind at my back. Ouch! You must resist the temptation to change the radius of the circle. Make a careful judgment about how far out you can successfully complete the 360 degree turn, and put your eyes on the airspeed and slip indicators so the turn is perfect. If you are really going to hit, you're going to hit under control, which isn't as bad as spinning in. Even if well above the ridge and in no risk of actually striking it, you can find yourself blown back into the lee if you don't center the thermal and climb quickly in the first few turns.

Being drawn down behind a ridge isn't fun, even with the engine on, because you need extra speed to penetrate against the wind in order to regain the edge of the cliff. You can dive to gain the extra speed needed to punch through the downdrafts and turbulence. The last 50 yards may have a reversed flow which can instantly drop the airspeed, as mentioned before.

The technique of flying away from the ridge periodically to see what's out there is a fine, safe way to catch thermals. Go at least 500 feet ahead of the hill before circling in an upcurrent. If there are good surges of lift near the hill, make slow S-turns as you fly out away from the ridge. Stay at minimum speed to benefit from spending the most time in the upcurrent. If you are still climbing in good lift and far enough ahead of the slope, look back to decide if you can, in fact, make a full circle. Once you have decided to circle in the thermal, look at the airspeed and yaw string, not back at the hill. If the thermal is good enough to lift you quickly, the plane will soon be high enough that lee downcurrents will not be a problem. If the thermal is weak or you haven't been able to center it very well and you find the plane is drifting past the top of the ridge, turn and head upwind immediately. In a few minutes, there should be another thermal where that one came from. Make another try or go back to beating up and down the ridge.

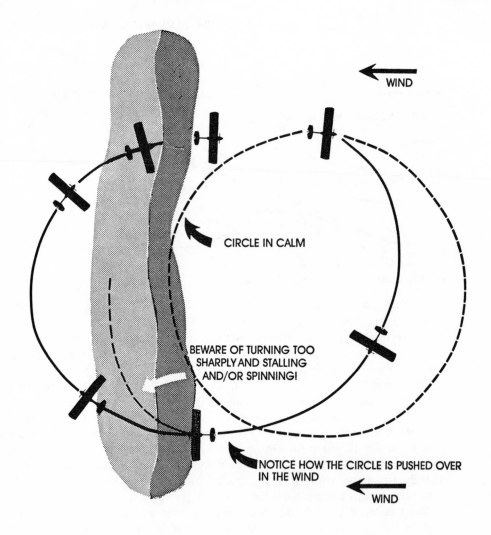

WIND

CIRCLE IN CALM

BEWARE OF TURNING TOO
SHARPLY AND STALLING
AND/OR SPINNING!

NOTICE HOW THE CIRCLE IS PUSHED OVER
IN THE WIND

WIND

Fig. 4-8. Circling near a ridge in wind.

Wind but No Lift

Sometimes the wind is blowing hard and there's very little lift, which is found only close to the ridge. It can be very baffling, especially when you've been experiencing fine upcurrents on days when the wind was very less. What's happening? How can the wind blow so hard without producing any lift? Is it going right through the hill? There are several conditions under which this happens. Perhaps the valley is filled with stable, cold air. The wind is hitting only the top edge of the ridge, which does not make enough deflection to result in good upcurrents.

Also common, is a reverse situation where an inversion has formed over the ridge. This clamps the lift down to the level below the warmer air above. In other words, there is a reversed lapse rate making for extremely stable air. It's a punk day for thermal soaring, as well as ridge soaring.

Waves

Under stable conditions, a wave can form on the lee side of a mountain or ridge. Just as water will make "stationary" waves over and behind a rock in a stream, so too will the air make waves over an obstruction. Best waves form in the stable air ahead of an approaching storm when there is a rapidly, increasing wind gradient. This means that a wind of 10 mph on the ground is 20 mph near the top of the ridge and 30 mph a little bit higher, and perhaps 40 mph above that. The faster belt of wind meets the "obstruction" of the air thrown up and down by the ridge, and builds up even higher. It's great to climb in a wave because the air is so

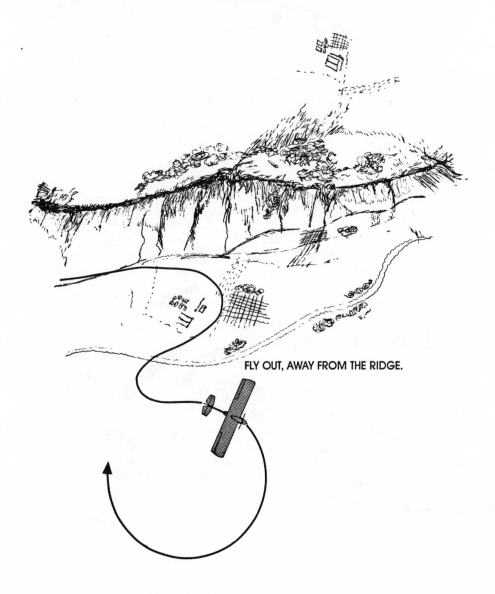

FLY OUT, AWAY FROM THE RIDGE.

Fig. 4-9. S-turn away from a ridge to stay in the upcurrent, until far enough away to safely circle without going into the cliff or the downcurrent.

81

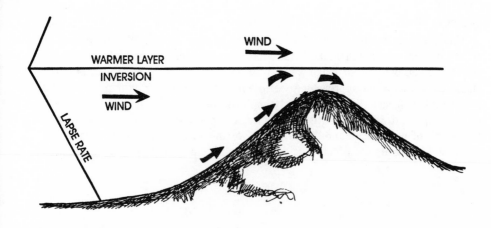

Fig. 4-10. Wind with poor or no lift occurs when an inversion squeezes the upcurrent down.

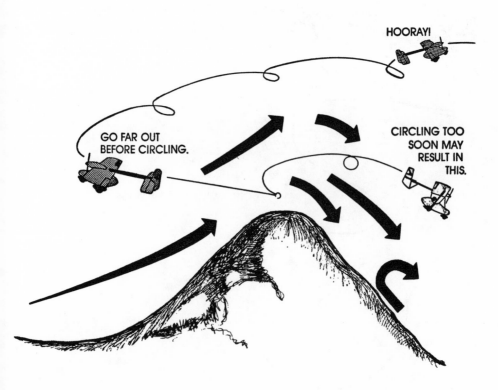

Fig. 4-11. Catching a thermal from ridge lift.

incredibly smooth once you are safely in the upcurrent. One glider pilot got up to 46,400 feet above sea level in a wave. I have been to 30,000 feet with oxygen and several times near 20,000 without. Once I was flying over Mono Lake in the down part of the wave which was so strong the water below me was frothing strangely. I headed for the road at the lee of the Sierras thinking that, if my motor-glider was pushed all the way down into the water, I'd have less distance to swim to shore. At the edge of the lake, the downflow changed to an equally strong up-current. With spoilers fully opened, I was smoothly and frighteningly carried to 19,000 feet before I angled downwind and dropped back to 11,000 before continuing on my way.

Vertical currents strong enough to fly a P-38 with the engines off, and turbulence that has almost exploded strong aircraft, is associated with the wave. The worst part of the wave is that it must be entered from below. There's a good chance you must pass through a rotor zone before reaching a smooth lift. This is where the upcurrent and downcurrents meet. It is sometimes marked by a row of raggedy clouds. If you watch them closely, you can see the rotary motion. They stand in the same place in a strong wind.

I have been in the rotor a few times. (The turbulence is unequalled!) Once I was pointing straight up yet the airspeed kept going higher and higher until past red line! A few seconds later the speed went to zero and I nosed down. Aimed at the ground, the airspeed was still reading zero! Yes, flying in a wave with an ultra-light would be quite an adventure. Yet, just as often, I have flown into very gentle lift so smooth I thought I was sitting on the ground.

Finding a Wave

You can best catch a wave from slope soaring when there are hills ahead of the ridge you are soaring. It can happen in two ways: a wave formed in the lee ahead of you may come to be in synchronism with the upcurrent from your hill. You'll be smoothly lifted two or three times higher than you ever were before under

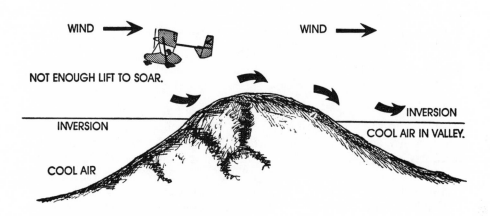

Fig. 4-12. An example of wind with no lift.

83

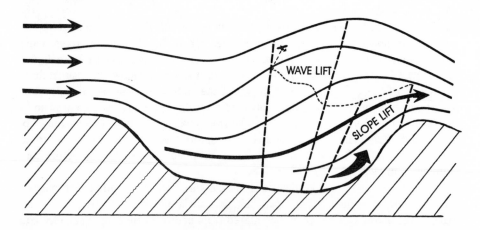

SOMETIMES, THE WAVE FROM THE HILLS ACROSS THE VALLEY CAN BE USED BY FLYING SLOWLY, STRAIGHT AHEAD FROM YOUR SOARING RIDGE.

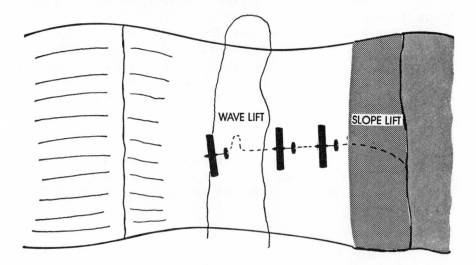

IN WAVES FOUND IN NORMAL WIND CONDITIONS, YOU MUST POINT ALMOST STRAIGHT INTO THE WIND TO HOLD POSITION IN THE LIFT AREA.

Fig. 4-13. Finding a wave safely

such winds at that ridge. Another wave experience can occur when you fly your ultralight into the wind ahead of the slope. About half way to the next range of hills you may notice a gentle climb. If an ultralight slows to almost zero ground speed stay nosed into the wind so you can keep position in the lift. Flying parallel may drift you back and out of the lift. When you turn back to the ridge you will find yourself far higher than the gang back at the original hill.

Heading downwind and after crossing a range of hills, being careful to go over at an angle to insure a way out, you may hit one or more rollers on the other side. Don't try to soar these rollers, they generally throw you up and down and are too small to climb in. Simply fly through them on course.

Summary of Ultralights and Slope Soaring

- Keep the yaw string centered and the wings level as you set a crab angle that will move the plane parallel to the cliff.
- All turns should be away from the slope.
- Crossing ridges, go at an angle to give yourself a way out.
- When going from the lee to the windward side close to a ridge, beware of wind reversal and/or downdrafts.
- Stay out of gullies and canyons on the lee side of the ridge.
- The lower half of very steep cliffs may have no lift, but plenty of turbulence.
- Always pass other aircraft on the ridge side when overtaking them.
- Fly the windward side of gullies and canyons only part way up, in order to stay out of turbulence from the adjoining ridges' lee side.
- Explore for thermals and waves by going well upwind of the ridge before making circles.

Chapter Five~
Ultralights and
Cloud Soaring

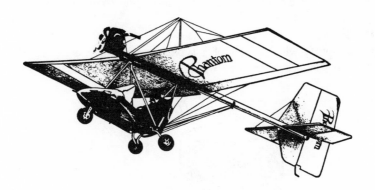

Ultralights, and Cloud Soaring

Cloudwatching, lying on a hillside in the summer sun, is considered for lovers and dreamers. But, you can learn a good deal about how to soar by observing clouds.

The Dew Point

Under the puffy white clouds of a typical summer day, are some of the best places to find thermal upcurrents. Why? As a thermal rises, it spreads out in the

THERMOMETER

CONDENSATION ON GLASS

Fig. 5-1. By comparing the ground temperature with the condensation temperature, and dividing by the lapse rate per thousand feet, you can estimate the height of the cloud base.

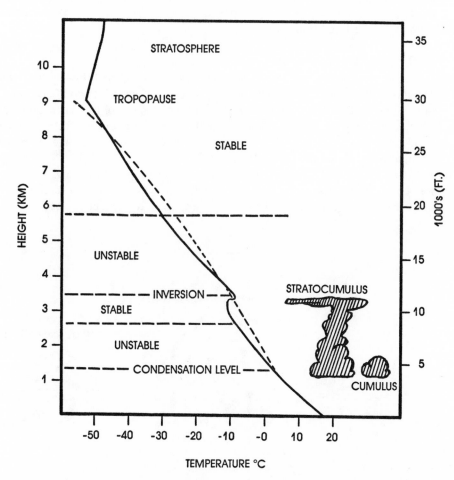

Fig. 5-2. The basic profile of the atmosphere.

thinner air away from the earth. Eventually, it is cooled enough that its water vapor clumps together into liquid. It is these very tiny droplets that can be seen as the white fog we call a cloud. The height where this happens depends on the amount of water in the air and the temperature. It's determined by the dew point.

You can estimate the cloud base height by finding the dew point. Put a thermometer in a cup of ice water. When you see the outside of the cup become wet from condensation, check the temperature. It may be 20 to 40 degrees cooler than the air around you. For this example, let's have a lapse rate of about ten degrees centigrade per thousand meters (or 3.5 degrees Fahrenheit for each thousand feet). If the cup started condensation on the outside when the liquid was 20 degrees colder, the cloud base would be (20 divided by 3.5 times 1,000 feet or) 5,700 feet high. The clouds are flat on the bottom because the water vapor begins condensing at the same temperature level.

If the dew point and the temperature on the ground are the same, or almost the same, fog would be expected. Sometimes clouds form when the air pressure, and therefore the temperature, drops suddenly. At the threshold of a big airport, watch the big jets land on a day with a low overcast. You will see fog pluming off the top of the wing because of the pressure drop as the wing pulls the air down above it. But back to lift under clouds.

Finding Lift Under Clouds

Clouds move with the wind so the thermals will be upwind. Fly upwind of a cumulus cloud about a 1,000 feet or more above the ground. If no lift is found, turn around and go directly downwind toward the cloud until lift is encountered, and begin circling. In the usual 10 to 15 mph wind, the slant of the thermal to the cloud would be about 4 to 1. So, if the cloud base is a mile up, you could expect to find the thermal four miles upwind.

Use polaroid sunglasses with a tan or brown lens for cloudwatching. You may see the slight haziness and tiny puffs of white just as the thermal reaches dew point and begins condensing. This is the best time to contact lift because the

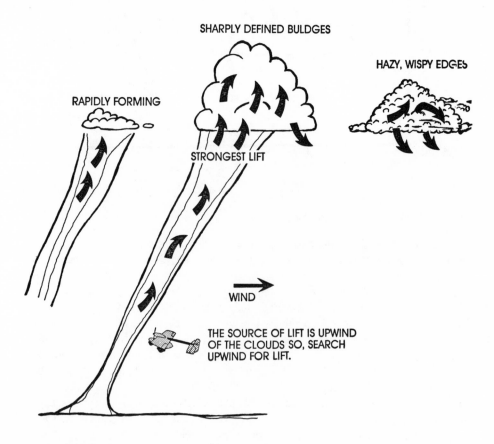

Fig. 5-3. The birth, life and death of a cumulus cloud.

thermal is probably extending all the way from the ground. Soon the cloud becomes easily visible and a well defined flat base is topped with sharply edged bulges. The cloud is now mature and a good bet for lift. At this stage, the thermal from which it is feeding may have drawn in all the hot air around it, then pulled away from the ground, so that the lift does not go down very low. The pilot must then get up underneath to climb. In five or ten minutes a cloud may begin to die. The edges become less distinct, then ragged and finally the cloud melts away.

Since thermals are upwind and below the cloud, the windward edge of the cloud is a likely place to find the lift. I have seen movies of cumulus clouds forming and dissipating. When the pictures are taken ten seconds apart and projected at a normal speed (so the entire cloud forms and dies in a half minute), a distinct rolling action can be seen. The windward side shoots up and the lee side goes down. Another "old pilot's" tale that works for me is to look for lift on the sunny side of the cloud.

As you fly along and feel the boost of the upcurrent, begin your smooth circles and your ultralight will rise toward the cloud. Cloud base can be approached quickly, so stay along the edge. Then you can fly away if there's any chance of being pulled into it.

Cloud Streets

After lazing around the edges and exploring the corners, you can fly to the next cloud. Buzzing along at partial power or quietly gliding, you can reach the cloud

BY RUNNING ALONG BELOW THE CLOUD STREET, WONDERFUL PERFORMANCE CAN BE HAD.

Fig. 5-4. In certain wind conditions and lapse rates, the clouds will arrange themselves in long rows known as cloud streets.

and be pushed, or drawn, to its base before heading off again. It is quiet, fun and very inexpensive flying. Sometimes the clouds form in long rows called streets. This is great for long glides along the edge. Get up close to the base, find the upwelling side, and cruise along with or without power. "Streeting" doesn't usually occur until later in the afternoon but can be used for long pleasant flights home or ending cross countries much farther than you would ordinarily have fuel for. Circling is not necessary. Just pull up and slow down in the lift to gain altitude, then nose down and pick up speed when the lift weakens and you can make good time cross country.

Summary of Ultralights and Cloud Soaring
- Go upwind of clouds to find lift.
- Watch for newly forming clouds.
- Solid looking puffy bulges are good lift clouds.
- Go away before too close to the base of the cloud.
- Porpoise when flying along cloud streets.

Chapter Six~
Ultralights, Shearlines
and Convergence Zones

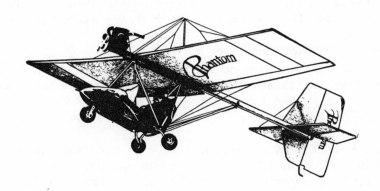

Ultralights, Shearlines and Convergence Zones

A surprisingly common, but seldom understood and under used soaring condition is what I call a shearline. It is also called a convergence zone and in some cases the sea breeze front. They can make for very interesting ultralight soaring flights.

Reasons for Convergence Zones

A shearline is the convergence zone between different air masses. Often there is a wind shift of 45 to 180 degrees at the line. I am most familiar with the Elsinore Shearline, and Southern California in general, having done many cross country soaring flights in gliders and my motorglider, as well as research using an instrumented 40 hp Piper Cub.

Lake Elsinore Valley is a popular flying site for powered ultralights, glider ultralights, and sailplanes. It owes much of its soaring to the action of the shearline. It is 56 miles from Los Angeles and 22 miles northeast of the Pacific shore, but separated by the Santa Ana Mountains which range from 2,000 to 6,000 feet above sea level.

In a typical spring, summer or, in particular, during the fall, a high pressure region is fairly stationary over the Pacific Ocean off the coast of California. The clockwise flow of the high pressure area creates winds that blow from the north to the southeast down the coast of California. The wind curls around Point Arguello and pushes into the Los Angeles Basin, helping create its infamous inversion. The cool, moist air sits under the hot, dry, clear air of the desert.

As the day progresses, the inland valleys and deserts become much hotter than

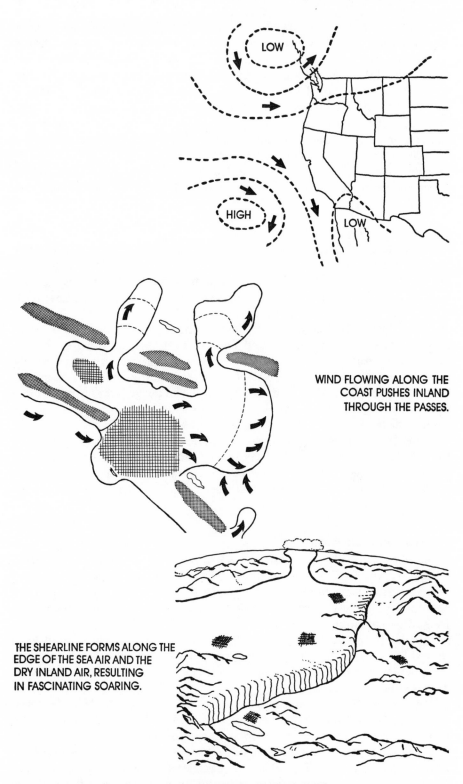

WIND FLOWING ALONG THE COAST PUSHES INLAND THROUGH THE PASSES.

THE SHEARLINE FORMS ALONG THE EDGE OF THE SEA AIR AND THE DRY INLAND AIR, RESULTING IN FASCINATING SOARING.

Fig. 6-1. The typical spring weather pattern along the west coast.

the coast. The heat means less dense air, as explained in the section on thermals. The inland low pressure starts pulling the cooler air toward it. It pushes through the Santa Ana Pass and, by afternoon you can see the wall of hazy air slowly approaching Lake Elsinore. Sometimes a row of raggedy cumulus marks the edge. By 4 p.m., it moves past the lake. There is a sudden shift in direction from southeast to northwest and the speed increases from 8 mph to 18 mph. The ultralights that flock on the northeast shore have learned to be weary of the sudden wind increases and change, as well as the turbulent dust devils snaking sideways along the edge of the shearline. This same situation creates shearlines not only in the Elsinore Valley but all across the Riverside plain, San Fernando Valley, and the passes leading to the desert such as: Cajon Pass, Mint Canyon, and Banning Pass.

How to Fly the Shearline

If you see the shearline approaching, you can fly toward it at an angle until you begin feeling the gusty turbulence. The lift is on the clearest side. Circle in the little bumps and try to find the strongest parts of the lift. Sometimes there are large, discrete thermals rising up the convergence line, while at other times the lift is almost too ragged and mixed up to center well.

I have flown in the shearline with other gliders and we ofttimes find ourselves circling alongside one another spaced only 50 to 100 yards apart, each of us convinced our part of the shearline is better. After climbing as high as you can, fly along the edge of the line being careful to keep the clear air on one side and the hazy air on the other. When flying along the line, you can go for many miles, often without circling, by slowing in the upcurrents and gliding more quickly in the down currents.

If you begin sinking and can't seem to find the lift, you have probably gone too far into the hazy side. So, angle back out toward the clear air. After flying the shearline a few times, you can develop an almost intuitive sense of where to position your plane to be in the lift and when to circle in thermals surging up the line.

Where to Find Shearlines

Shearlines can be found all over the world. Some places to look might be near a large lake which will develop an evening breeze toward itself, after the land cools off. An ocean breeze front will occur during the day when the ground heats up again and pulls the cool air from over the lake. In both situations, good lift is likely at the convergence zone.

Shearlines lines are particularly noticeable where a mass of air is forced to go through a valley or pass and becomes concentrated. In California, almost every valley leading toward the sea creates a shearline where the sea breeze meets the drier land air.

Near Marfa, Texas a marvelous, huge shearline runs north where the moist Gulf air converges with the drier air mass from New Mexico. The Great Lakes also create shearline conditions consistently, as do most large lakes.

I have flown almost 300 miles on a desert shearline stretching from Victorville to the Colorado River and on along the Lake Mead boundary. To discover your own shearlines, try to figure out the pattern of the winds near your flying site. Be

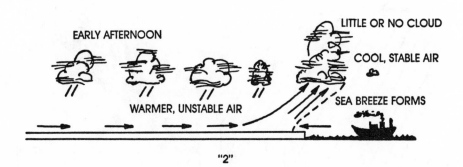

EARLY MORNING, UNTIL MID-DAY

PREVAILING WIND OFF-SHORE   THERMALS FORMING CLOUDS

"1"

EARLY AFTERNOON

LITTLE OR NO CLOUD

COOL, STABLE AIR

WARMER, UNSTABLE AIR

SEA BREEZE FORMS

"2"

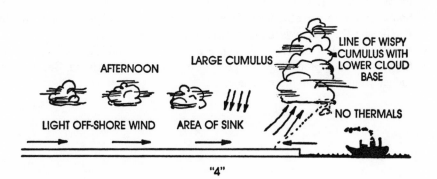

AFTERNOON WITH STRONG OFF-SHORE WIND

BELT OF LIFT

"3"

AFTERNOON

LARGE CUMULUS

LINE OF WISPY CUMULUS WITH LOWER CLOUD BASE

LIGHT OFF-SHORE WIND   AREA OF SINK

NO THERMALS

"4"

Fig. 6-2. The daily development of the sea breeze front.

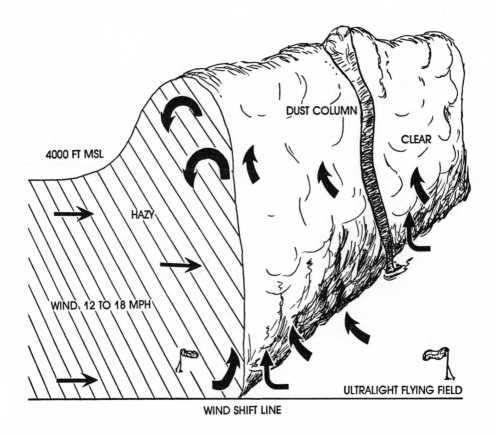

4000 FT MSL

DUST COLUMN

CLEAR

HAZY

WIND, 12 TO 18 MPH

ULTRALIGHT FLYING FIELD

WIND SHIFT LINE

Fig. 6-3. A cross section through the Elsinore shearline.

aware of wind shifts and watch for a different texture or visibility. Try to look for perhaps a faint row of clouds. They may mark the unseen boundary of a lift inspiring shearline.

Summary of Ultralights, Shearlines and Convergence Zones

- Any great differences in surface, such as lakes, valleys, forests and oceans, can cause local air masses to form shearlines.
- Southern California shearlines develop because of the high pressure over the Pacific and the heat low that is created inland during the day.
- Fly along the clear air side of the convergence zone to find lift.
- Be wary of an approaching shearline when you're on the ground. Get ready for sudden wind shift and more gustiness.

Chapter Seven~ Ultralights and Cloud Safety

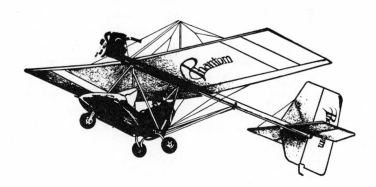

Ultralights and Cloud Safety

In late summer afternoons, what seemed to be a fine little cumulus when you started climbing may have spread and developed almost explosively by the time you have climbed to its base. Little may you suspect it now goes to 18,000 feet. The lift may be so strong the bottom of the cloud is bell shaped because the warm rising air is pushing it up. The lift can be well over 1,000 feet per minute and you can be drawn up into the inverted bowl. Soon you can only see directly below. You may try to head away and instead go into the cloud.

It does no good to exhort pilots to stay out of the clouds and recount tragedies of planes broken up and coming out the bottom in tiny pieces. It may be scary, but it does not make a safer pilot by saying never go into a big cumulus on purpose without gyro instruments.

Remember, flying in clouds is against Federal Air Regulations because other airplanes can't see you. That problem is very slight compared to the serious possibility of losing control and breaking the plane from over-stress. These suggestions are based on ways some pilots have survived having accidentally gone into clouds. It is better to learn about them and practice in clear air, then swear you are never going into a cloud. Knowing what can happen and what can be done to survive should make any pilot even more wary of getting in a position where his plane might go into the clouds.

Flying Blind

When an ultralight is in a cloud, the pilot can't recover from any turn, spin, or

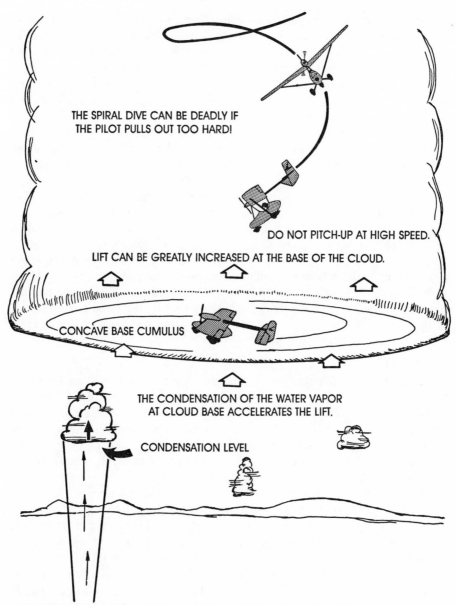

THE SPIRAL DIVE CAN BE DEADLY IF THE PILOT PULLS OUT TOO HARD!

DO NOT PITCH-UP AT HIGH SPEED.

LIFT CAN BE GREATLY INCREASED AT THE BASE OF THE CLOUD.

CONCAVE BASE CUMULUS

THE CONDENSATION OF THE WATER VAPOR AT CLOUD BASE ACCELERATES THE LIFT.

CONDENSATION LEVEL

THE LAST FEW HUNDRED FEET BELOW THE CLOUD CAN HAVE UNEXPECTEDLY POWERFUL UPCURRENTS THAT ARE DIFFICULT TO FLY AWAY FROM IN TIME TO ESCAPE.

Fig. 7-1. Some details about clouds.

other attitudes because there is no way to tell when the plane is straight and level. You could be doing loops and never know it because the only sensation would be a positive G at the bottom and less at the top. When the light G's at the top of the loop occur, the pilot feels the plane must be diving so the ship is pulled up, thus completing the loop. When the airspeed reads low, the pilot may nose down. The airspeed increases but the lag between the pilot's control input and the actual speed is a few seconds. The plane may either overspeed or stall before corrections to the pitch may be made.

I tried flying my motorglider with a shield over my head, so only the airspeed, compass and altimeter could be seen. My friend, Charlie Webber, watched for other aircraft and stayed in contact by radio. I found I could fly very well by listening to the sound of the motor and watching the airspeed for about as long as I wanted. But, the plane made wide circles while climbing over 4,000 feet in about 10 minutes! If I put the plane into a spiral dive or a simple stall, it was impossible to get it back flying smoothly without pulling off my hood. I proved it is possible to fly blind without a gyro horizon or a turn-gyro indicator if you know your plane very well so you know enough to leave it alone and it doesn't speed up. However, in the turbulence of a cumulus cloud you would probably end up in a spiral dive.

If you go into a cloud, the plane will keep level for awhile under its own stability while you sit in the whiteness, eyes glued to the yaw string and airspeed. A few bumps shove you up and down and the compass turns. Although I've heard of pilots flying a compass heading to get out, I find it is conducive to overcontrol trying to chase it. So, don't try to steer with the compass in a cloud. The lag is too great, as well as the wild swinging that occurs when the compass card is not level with the earth. You sit thinking everything is at least reasonably alright when the speed goes up a little. After pulling the nose up slightly, the speed drops off. Two or three excursions of the airspeed and you've gotten the speed back each time. Fine, you think you've got it licked.

The Spiral Dive

Next thing you know the speed is up again so you pull the nose up. Instead of the airspeed dropping, it seems not only to be resisting going down but, it is actually going up! G's push you down into the seat. The roar of the air through the rigging is louder and louder, the engine is howling. "Slow it down, slow it down!" Your brain screams and you pull even harder to get the nose up. The wings are shuddering, the wires are taut, the wings bend more, the plane shudders and flutters - - - bang! What to do? Open your parachute.

The first part of the story was fine. Don't move things around. The engine should be shut off or brought back to idle. Watch the yaw string and keep the speed as low as you can. When you realize the speed is increasing and the G loads are building, you should recognize the plane is in a spiral dive. It will take great willpower, but stop trying to pull the nose up. Hold the control bar or control stick in neutral. Actually look at it to make sure it is in the right position. Look out at the tail to double check. If you just hold it there, your chances of coming out of the cloud in one piece are better, because most ultralights are so draggy they will not speed up enough to be destroyed by flutter. As long as the aircraft is not maneuvered suddenly, it may be sturdy enough to survive high speed. In a cumulus cloud however, sudden gusts or turbulence can break a plane in a terminal speed spiral dive, so it is better to stop the turn.

Recovery

How? You don't even know which way the plane is turning. Take a guess. Try a little bank one way and back to neutral. Watch the airspeed. If nothing happens, bank it again in the same direction, perhaps a little longer. If you get a speed increase, you know you have banked even more into a spiral dive so bank the other way a little bit until the speed drops off.

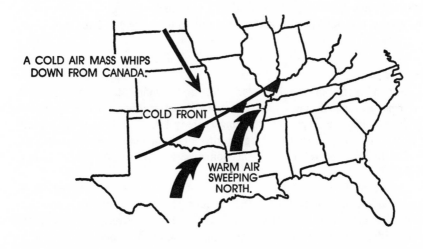

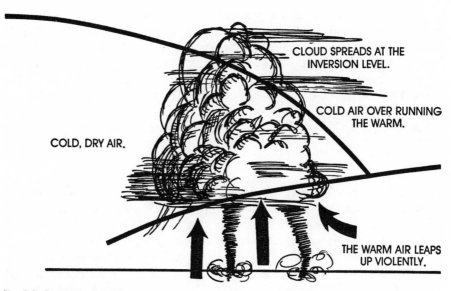

Fig. 7-2. Tornado conditions.

As the plane comes out of the spiral dive it will tend to go into a stall, so try nosing down a little when you guess it is about ready. You can feel the deceleration, even though the airspeed may lag slightly.

With conventional controls, try to hold the plane in a spin. Hold the stick back all the way, throttle back and full rudder. A spinning airplane will not break up! Your plane may not be a good spinner, so practice spins and recovery to see if it will hold a ten turn spin without winding up in a spiral dive. A good ultralight should spin steadily with a predictable entry and recovery. When you come out of the cloud, whether in a controlled spin or a spiral dive, be sure to smoothly and slowly make the recovery. Many pilots have broken their airplanes not in the cloud but when they came out the bottom, saw they were in a steep spiral dive and, in a panic, pulled out too quickly. A spiral dive is not so dangerous as pulling out too hard.

Thunderstorms

Many ultralights fly in the Mid-West and East, where spring and summer thunderstorms and squall lines are common. Understanding something about handling this condition is important to being a safer pilot. Some thunderstorms are local, the result of an upcurrent developing into a cumulus cloud which continues to grow due to the heat released by the condensation of the water at the dew point level.

At condensation, five hundred calories per cc of water is released. This amounts to millions and millions of BTUs for the amount of air rising in a good thermal column. With a good lapse rate, the cloud will build explosively and can reach 50,000 feet. Rain falling and the cold air brings downdrafts which could make a local "cold" front.

Squall Lines

Sometimes a line of storms will build with a wall of cold air dropping out, pushing warm air up ahead of it. This is a squall line and it may be 50 to 300 miles long. The largest and most dramatic occur when a mass of cool, dry air from Canada meets a warm, moist swath of air coming up from the Gulf of Mexico. The meeting ground is more often in Kansas or Oklahoma but can by anywhere in the Mid-West. The cool air may rush down so fast it will overrun the hot, moist air from the South. The hot air tries to rise through the cool mass as the heavy cold air drops through the lighter mass below. It's like pulling the plug on a gigantic bath tub!

Tornadoes

Tornadoes form like upside down whirlpools. Where there are sudden changes in wind direction, and massive down spurts, tornadoes can form. An ultralight would be destroyed in seconds!

It was thought the suction in the center of the spinning tornado was the cause of its destruction, but the reduced pressure in the center of the tornado is only four pounds per square foot. The real cause of the destruction is the powerful winds around the edge of the tornado. A 200 mile an hour wind puts a pressure of over 100 pounds per square foot on any flat object in its path.

If you see a storm coming, you can disassemble your machine and put it in a safe place out of the wind. But, if you're flying on a typically hot, muggy day, the haze may be such that you can't see a squall line approaching. It happened to me one well remembered June day near Chicago, Illinois.

Storm Flight

I was gliding in the open cockpit of the University of Illinois Glider Club's little machine. It was four in the afternoon on a perfectly calm, hot, humid day. I had two tows but only glided smoothly to the ground. On the third, I felt an

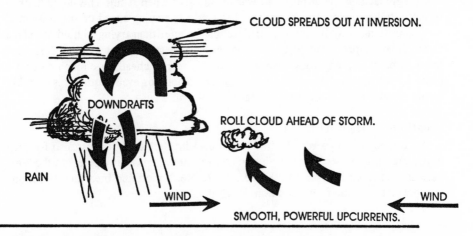

CLOUD SPREADS OUT AT INVERSION.

DOWNDRAFTS

ROLL CLOUD AHEAD OF STORM.

RAIN

WIND

WIND

SMOOTH, POWERFUL UPCURRENTS.

Fig. 7-3. Cross section of a squall line showing area to stay in front of.

upcurrent and circled to make the first altitude gain I had ever done. At 3,000 feet it became cold in that open cockpit because I had no shirt on. I looked out and instead of the airport below, saw a wall of white and the grey rain of a storm that had appeared from nowhere. I headed away toward the north side of Chicago, in company with the Purdue University glider. He out distanced me and eventually landed in a playground.

In the little low speed glider I was flying, by the time I approached the same spot the storm caught up to me and drew me higher. It was very smooth, I couldn't even feel the lift. I had studied about cold fronts and thunderstorms in old books and recognized the roll cloud ahead of the main storm, and was determined to stay out of it. By moving ahead, I was able to overfly Chicago and go on to Indiana. The cold front was not a straight line but weaved in and out. By flying at 34 mph, just far enough away to keep from sinking but not close enough to be swept up, I was able to keep going almost five hours.

At one point, I went into one of the "bay" formations in the roll cloud to keep my position, with the storm formed ahead of me. The little Schweizer 1-19 was lifted to 6,000 feet. The storm closed in all around and below. I was in a clear box at the moment so, while still level, I pulled up. When it stalled, I kept the stick tightly back and held full rudder and it entered a tight spin. I held the spin firmly as it dropped into the clouds. In the whiteness, it seemed the plane was straight and level but I kept the controls in spin position until the whirling ground appeared from the midst below. I flew through rain until I was back out in front.

At sunset, I glided ahead of the storm to land in a small field 109 miles from my takeoff. I was able to tie the plane to a fence before the storm, which by now was almost dead, arrived.

It was a dangerous flight, not in its actuality, only in its potential, had I been drawn into the storm and lost control. Back at the home field, it had been very dangerous with rain and hail combined with strong winds, so everyone made heroic efforts to keep the gliders from being damaged. For me it was a marvelous adventure and one that certainly could have been done by an ultralight. I'm not recommending every pilot try squall line flying, of course, but in my case I never saw the storm approaching the airport and was at 400 feet when it hit! This could happen to any ultralight pilot, and knowing what to do — staying ahead of the roll cloud and keep flying away from the storm — could be safer than trying to hold the plane down in an unprotected place. At the onset of a storm, violent windshifts and hail can be more dangerous than using the lift to run ahead far enough to find a place to put the ship. Perhaps a hanger at an airport, or even a quick disassembly would be safer than a landing in the face of a storm.

Breathing at High Altitude

An ultralight can go very high if it is drawn into a cloud. It must also fly high if you are on a cross country trying to go over mountains. Many places in the West have ground levels of over 14,000 feet. Therefore, a modified breathing technique is important for good flying and even survival.

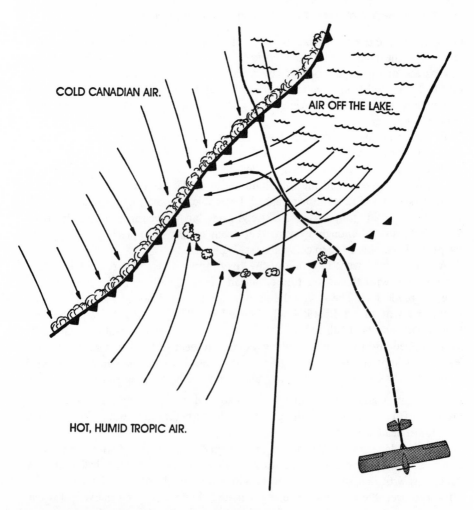

Fig. 7-4. Squall line conditions during a storm flight. A common condition that exists near lake Michigan, resulting in violently good lift.

106

Lack of Oxygen

A few hours over 10,000 feet above sea level for most of us lowlanders will be enough to produce a powerful headache. While there is the same percentage of oxygen up high as there is at sea level, the density is much lower, and oxygen does not go into the blood as easily. If you're accustomed to high altitude, it won't bother you because the body makes extra red blood cells to take in oxygen to make up for the lower air density. I spent three weeks flying a motorglider to Paraguay during the course of which I flew at 9,000 to 13,000 feet to go over storms in Columbia and clouds in Ecuador. I found I didn't need oxygen until I spent over an hour at 16 to 17,000 feet working thermals trying to cross the Andes Mountains. I discovered the need for oxygen when I couldn't hear my stereo headset no matter how loud I turned it up. I put on the oxygen mask, sucked in two breaths, and the music suddenly increased in volume. I reached La Paz, Bolivia, and stayed a few days. At 12,000 feet the city didn't bother me as much as the tourists walking about weak kneed and blue faced, only because I had spent many hours flying at high altitude.

The children at that altitude play soccer and dash around on bicycles, the same as anywhere else. If you go to 12,000 feet and try running around, you can see how adaptable they are. You could conceivably live at 12,000 feet for a week to practice for the possibility of a high flight in an ultralight. However, not only is this impracticable but your high altitude conditioning would be lost in only a week back at sea level.

If very high in a thermal, perhaps over 14,000 feet, you will find it is almost impossible to tell the effect of oxygen starvation because the brain is the first organ to be affected. How can you comprehend what's going on if you can't think? Some experts say, "Look at your fingertips to see if the color under the nails is turning bluish, to indicate lack of air." This sounds fine except you can't think well enough to decide whether they are blue or not and to what degree.

The effects of altitude vary between people. I get an uneasy feeling of impending doom called "Dreads" while others have the same symptoms as being "Drunk." I notice my peripheral vision pulls in about 30 degrees so it seems as if I can only see clearly straight ahead. The sound of the wind becomes very quiet and the cold of high altitude is not so noticeable. I see little "blips," like the stars you see if you bump your head. Little dots pop up in front of my eyes and disappear.

Grunt Breathing

A good way to check your condition is by doing what the Navy calls "Grunt Breathing." Take a deep breath, holding your mouth closed, and grunt to pressurize your lungs. You will immediately hear better and the vision out of the corner of your eyes will clear. The affect lasts only a few seconds but by grunt breathing you can see how much you change immediately after pressurizing your lungs.

I've been to over 20,000 feet several times without oxygen, accidently of course, and have used grunt breathing to keep out of trouble. Another important rule is "Never make decisions over 14,000 without oxygen." Decide when down low what your going to do, such as your compass heading, and plan for the next hour. Up high, stick single mindedly to the plan. Trying to think brilliant, new ideas after a while at high altitude, can result in mistakes which you do not realize until low again. You might ask yourself, "What am I doing going in this direction, when I was intending to go in the opposite way over the mountains? At 14,000 feet a new

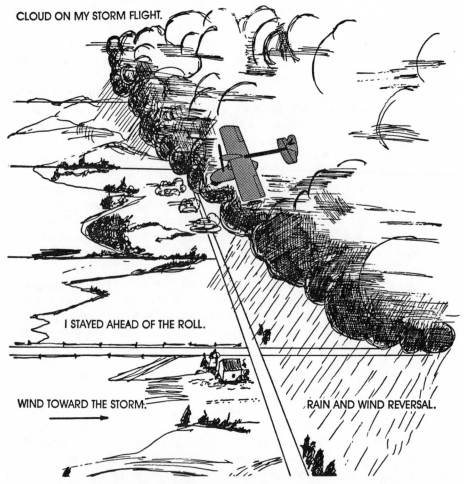

CLOUD ON MY STORM FLIGHT.

I STAYED AHEAD OF THE ROLL.

WIND TOWARD THE STORM. →

RAIN AND WIND REVERSAL.

Fig. 7-5. The storm flight described in the text.

plan probably seemed an incredibly clever idea.

The bitter cold at high altitude can be more harmful to your flying than lack of oxygen. So, in an open ultralight I would not go very high. These hints are ways to check yourself to lessen the danger of trouble in case you get caught in a wave.

Once, I was thrown to 19,800 feet over Mono Lake, California with full spoilers on, and survived. If you are drawn into a cloud and are having a desperate time, remember grunt breathing to give you a few seconds of clear thought at a time when you need it most.

Summary of Ultralights and Cloud Safety
- The stronger the lift, the sooner you must leave.
- Pulling too many "G's" will break the plane.
- A spin or a gentle spiral is the safest way out.
- Late afternoon cumulus can build into thunderstorms.
- Stay ahead of a squall line roll cloud.
- The brain quits first at altitude.
- "Grunt Breathe" to check your condition.
- Stay away from very strong weather.

Chapter Eight~
Cross-Country
in an Ultralight

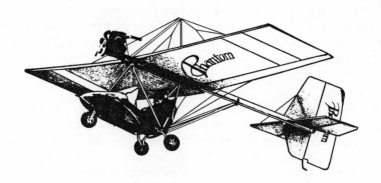

Cross-Country in an Ultralight

The art of cross country flying combines many skills. Using lift, knowledge of the winds, and good judgment in landing are all extremely important. Navigation in ultralights is a different kind of skill. It's different than the feelings, understandings and maneuverings needed to fly. It is a highly specialized kind of "orienteering" while in the air.

Landing Out

The major skill needed when flying cross country in an ultralight is being able to land in strange fields. An inexperienced pilot has no idea of the problems involved in landing out. Although the low speeds of ultralights make serious injury unlikely, there's no sense spoiling a good flight by damaging the landing gear, propeller, or wings. Disturbing private property, by poor choice of fields, and tearing down TV antennas, breaking telephone wires, or scaring animals and people makes nothing but a bad name for the sport. You should be an expert at landing out even though you may never plan to make a cross country flight. Remember, your engine could quit at any time!

Flying a Pattern

Start landing out practice by flying around your home field in a rectangle about 300 feet up. Climb out straight, turn left, fly alongside your runway downwind, then turn left again, slow the engine and glide down for a landing. When you are able to put it down and stop exactly where you want to, every time, start modifying the pattern. Begin the landing approach higher, a tight turn to final, or very low with a little throttle on.

Practice by stopping the engine to get an idea of the glide range and control feel without wind from the propeller. The safest technique for a landing is known as the "high-energy-approach." It is used by sailplane pilots as well as the NASA Space Shuttle astronauts. When done in an ultralight, it means the plane is in position for the landing higher than usual and dived at cruise speed or higher, aiming at a point 20 yards short of the landing spot. You can slow the plane and turn its speed into extra distance if you are going to fall short. If it appears the plane is too high, dive even faster.

The drag at high speed is much greater so the plane will not pick up speed as much as it will lose altitude. When a few feet above the ground, level off and continue to let the speed dissipate until the plane drops for a smooth landing. Look far ahead and try to keep the plane flying level to touchdown. In most ultralights, the extra carry of the high energy approach will not extend the flight more than a couple dozen yards past the leveling off place.

To see if you are going to be short or long, sight along a mark on the plane and your landing spot, assuming you always keep the same pitch angle. If it is moving down, in reference to the mark, it means you are going to go past. If it is moving up in your vision, the plane will be falling short, in which case you must nose up, and slow down to increase your gliding range. Much practice will give you a sense of where to level off and allow the speed to bleed off, touching down exactly where you wish. Remember, this is not "ground effect." The whole idea of the high energy approach is to give yourself extra gliding distance when you need it by trading speed into distance. If you are approaching slowly, see that your landing spot is moving up, and be aware that you're falling short. There's not much you can do to extend your glide with the engine off.

Airports Without a Tower

Before we go into the details of landing in strange fields, let's plan that your engine will never stop and you will use regular, small, lightplane fields. It's perfectly safe to land at airports without control towers if you do not bother or conflict with the regular traffic. The standard pattern for light planes is a box with all turns to the left, with one edge over the runway facing nearest the wind. Entry into this pattern calls for a 45 degree turn into the downwind leg at 800 feet with spacing between airplanes maintained by slowing down if too close to the plane ahead or speeding up if someone is too close to your tail.

A slow ultralight would be in conflict if it tried using the standard pattern mixed in with regular airplanes. You could follow the airport's helicopter pattern if you knew what it was for each airport, but lacking that, make a pattern similar to the other planes so that no one gets angry at the "ignorant ultralight pilots who don't make a pattern." This approach will look the same but, in fact, will be quite different. The ultralight pattern should be lower and smaller than that of the regular planes. Stay at about 300 feet as you enter the downwind leg and 100 feet to one side of the runway you intend to land on — it's called the "active." Check ahead for planes on base or turning to final, and especially look far ahead for someone on a long final. If everything is all clear, turn a short base over the end of the runway to final. Stay alongside the active runway until about 10 feet up.

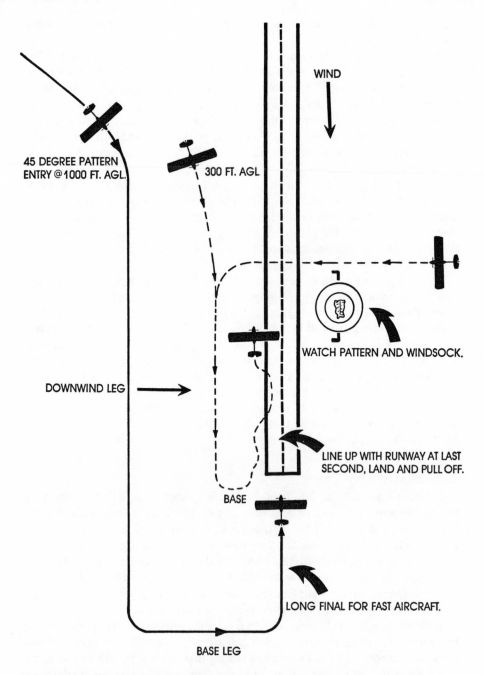

WIND

45 DEGREE PATTERN
ENTRY @1000 FT. AGL.

300 FT. AGL.

DOWNWIND LEG

WATCH PATTERN AND WINDSOCK.

LINE UP WITH RUNWAY AT LAST
SECOND, LAND AND PULL OFF.

BASE

LONG FINAL FOR FAST AIRCRAFT.

BASE LEG

Fig. 8-1. When landing at an airport where the tower is not operating or there is no tower, use a smaller pattern and the "safety final" to keep from being over run by faster aircraft.

Check again for landing traffic, rock your wings, move over to the edge of the runway and land on the side edge of the runway. As soon as you are slow, pull off the runway and taxi on the grass or taxiway to wherever you plan to park, get fuel, or whatever.

By making your pattern inside and lower than the other planes, you are always where they can see you. Yet, the pattern is similar to what the regular planes fly so they know you are approaching to land.

Most mid-air collisions occur during final approach to the runway. Why? Pilots look all around the sky in the pattern for other traffic. On downwind they look both ways and also look carefully as they turn base to see if anyone else is on final, before turning themselves. Once committed to the final approach and landing, the flyer has a mental "cleared-to-land" attitude and is looking straight ahead concentrating on the coming landing.

Many pilots have been told time and again by instructors that they should have a stabilized final approach with no changes in airspeed or turns, with an aiming spot at the center of the runway.

I think this is wrong—here's why. Planes slide into one another when flying alongside, or a plane with a wing on the bottom drops onto a high wing type. Those on the ground often have seen the planes approaching alongside for a good distance, yet the pilots may not see each other because they aren't looking while on final.

During World War II in Belgium, two loads of British fighter pilots died when the small transports carrying them arrived at the base at the same time. Their comrades at the airport watched horrified as the two planes came together from their long steady approaches.

A glider pilot friend of many years died when his beautiful fiberglass glider and the towplane ran together on final approach. The towplane was thinking of dropping the towline for the next glider, and my friend was concentrating on his landing spot, when they stuck their wings through one another.

Approaching Chino one day I called the tower for landing instructions and was told "Runway 26, report one mile out." At one mile I called and heard "Cleared-

As it happened, a Beechcraft Bonanza either overrode my second call, or me his. At any rate, the "Cleared-to-land" was apparently meant for the Bonanza. I was, as usual, just to the side of the centerline on final when the Bonanza sped past not 20 yards away. I talked to the pilot later. "No, I never saw any airplanes on my approach," he said, "why, anything wrong?" He was, as I believe every pilot is, blind to other planes when concentrating on the runway ahead.

The Safety Final

Since the long stable approach is the one most likely to involve a mid-air collision, always stay to one side. Never line up with the centerline of the runway in your landing because that's where the other planes are aiming.

"The most important part of a landing is the nicely stabilized final glide." I strongly disagree! A pilot should be able to land out of a circling turn, make S-turns almost to touchdown, or change speed throughout the descent. Of course, all this is more difficult. It takes practice. But, what kind of a wimp pilot needs to set up an airliner approach before being able to make a good landing? What if the engine quits as you're leaving the field in a climbing turn? What if you're circling low over an interesting spot and the engine stops? Perhaps you are forced to do a turn in the last 100 feet to miss suddenly seen power lines. All of these situations require turns quickly and skillfully done.

I make wing rocking S-turns on final and smooth out only in the last few seconds, only because more airplanes are more likely to see this waggling, turning thing ahead of them. Maneuvering on final forces you away from concentrating on that landing spot ahead to the exclusion of everything else.

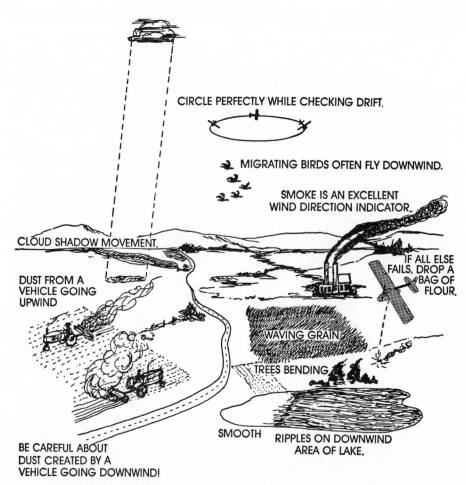

CIRCLE PERFECTLY WHILE CHECKING DRIFT.

MIGRATING BIRDS OFTEN FLY DOWNWIND.

SMOKE IS AN EXCELLENT WIND DIRECTION INDICATOR.

CLOUD SHADOW MOVEMENT.

IF ALL ELSE FAILS, DROP A BAG OF FLOUR.

DUST FROM A VEHICLE GOING UPWIND

WAVING GRAIN

TREES BENDING

SMOOTH RIPPLES ON DOWNWIND AREA OF LAKE.

BE CAREFUL ABOUT DUST CREATED BY A VEHICLE GOING DOWNWIND!

Fig. 8-2. Various ways to determine wind direction.

I have only been called on this once. When landing at Santa Monica Airport doing my little "raindance" on final, the tower said, "Hey, what kind of an approach is that?" I said, "That's my safety approach so other planes will notice, okay?" Answer, "Yea, it does look different all right." So I stress, practice your special ultralight pattern to stay lower inside the other planes. Make S-turns on final and always stay a wing span to one side of the centerline.

Field Landings

An airport has a wind sock, or airplanes are using the active runway, so you know which way to land. Many times in ultralight flying you will be coming down in an ordinary field with no runways, traffic, or wind sock.

Finding Wind Direction

Start by being aware of wind direction when you take off, in relation to the course you are planning to fly. Knowing the wind direction and looking for anything that will confirm what you already know, such as trees bending, flags waving, and smoke, is good practice. Often the wind changes, depending on the time of day and the part of the valley over which you're flying. There are usually downslope winds at sunset and upslope winds in the heat of the day.

Cloud Shadows

Sometimes the wind at the level in which you are flying is not the same as that near the ground. Cloud shadows are a good sign of the winds aloft. Watch the edge of a cloud shadow for at least 30 seconds to get an idea of upper wind direction and strength.

Smoke

Smoke is one of the best indicators of surface winds as it is easily seen and its slant can tell much about speed, stability, and direction. If the smoke is going skyward vertically, it should be calm. Whereas, leaving its source almost parallel to the ground shows high wind. If the smoke waves up and down, it may trace the turbulence in the air.

Dust may look like smoke but it is more confusing because it may be rising from the passage of a car on a dirt road or a tractor in a field. You can get the impression the wind is going opposite from reality. For example, the appearance may be that the car or tractor is heading into a gentle wind, when it is actually in a strong tailwind because the dust plume is moving along behind it at slightly less ground speed. Wait until the vehicle changes direction to see what the dust is doing.

Watch for flags, clothes drying (if that's possible in this age of dryers), bending trees, and the flow of wind making crops wave, can all be indicators. Water shows wind streaks. Sometimes even the smallest pond can show wind patterns at a great distance, if the reflection is just right. The upwind side of a lake or pond will show less wind streaks than a downwind side. If you can see nothing in the air, try

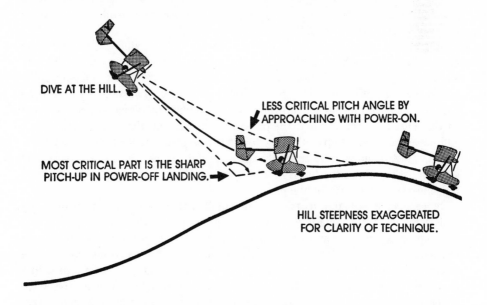

DIVE AT THE HILL.

LESS CRITICAL PITCH ANGLE BY APPROACHING WITH POWER-ON.

MOST CRITICAL PART IS THE SHARP PITCH-UP IN POWER-OFF LANDING.

HILL STEEPNESS EXAGGERATED FOR CLARITY OF TECHNIQUE.

Fig. 8-3. Uphill landings can be very safe if you watch your airspeed and do not become confused by the slope of the hill and pull up too soon.

smooth circles to see which way the plane drifts or even drop a bag of flour to make a burst of dust before setting up a landing pattern.

Knowing the wind direction, even if you are flying high, is important. If the engine stops, glide downwind to look for landing places. You can cover a lot more ground than into the wind. When you are ready to land, of course, turn into the wind.

If the breeze is over 8 mph, always land into the wind to touch down at the slowest, and therefore, safest speed. In very calm air, consider the approach and slope of the land instead. It would be better to come in crosswind or in a slight downwind if it means an approach across a ditch or low fence, instead of high trees and power lines. Where to draw the line? That is purely in the area of indefinable "good judgment."

Hill Landing

Ignoring the slope of the land can make for unexpected trouble. On a hill approach, the tendency is to assume level ground, resulting in "leveling" off in a slight climb too soon and stalling. In mountainous country, it's very easy to have surrounding hills and valleys confuse your idea of the actual horizon. Pastures that appear perfectly level can be sloping at 5 degrees or more. Look far out at the bases of the hills to get an idea of the horizon and watch the airspeed.

Properly done, a landing and takeoff using a hill is the shortest and safest of all. You can stop in a much smaller distance going uphill. Takeoff is easy going downhill because the slope helps the plane accelerate, while giving you lots of height above the ground immediately. Aim into the wind, open the throttle, and swoop off.

Uphill landings are more difficult because touchdown is very nose high and the plane must be stopped where it won't roll back!

One of my friends landed his glider on a wet grassy hill near Elmira, New York. It was a perfect landing on a fine hill in an extremely short space. Then the all metal glider slipped back all the way down the hill, over an embankment, onto the highway and into the guardrail!

A good technique for a hill landing in an ultralight is aiming just below the rounded top of the hill. As the plane approaches, concentrate on your airspeed. Keep the engine on until just over the slope, then quickly start pitching up to match the angle of the hill. The speed will drop very quickly as soon as you throttle back, because you're pitched up the hill, even though the visual angle of descent to the hillside is very slight. If the plane starts to stop on the slope after landing, add power and drive it up to the very top so it won't slide back. If the engine is off, pull up must be done more suddenly and skillfully because the angle between the glide and the angle of the hill is often 30 degrees. If the wind is behind you, go up hill unless the wind is 15 to 20 mph.

In general, it is better to take off downhill with a tailwind instead of uphill against the wind. Deciding if the wind is very strong and whether the hill is gentle or steep takes judgment and practice. The surface and length of your landing spot can help you decide if the slope is very rough and the wind strong. You can be down and stopped short even on a slight uphill. If the ground is smooth with a good approach, landing downwind and uphill is no problem. The relative wind strength versus angle of slope and smoothness of surface are infinite factors that only experience can assess properly. Basically however, land uphill and take off downhill.

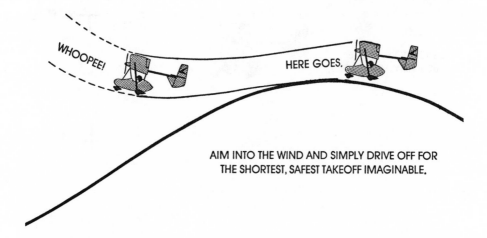

WHOOPEE!

HERE GOES.

AIM INTO THE WIND AND SIMPLY DRIVE OFF FOR
THE SHORTEST, SAFEST TAKEOFF IMAGINABLE.

Fig. 8-4. Taking off from a hill.

To assess slopes from the air is difficult because everything seems flat. Over stream beds, note the direction of water flow. Look for gulleys at the edges of fields. Water running off the downslope slide of the field will erode more visibly going toward a river and you can guess the land is sloping with your direction of travel. After crossing the river, the ground will be sloping against the direction of flight. Looking for signs of slope direction is a good habit because it helps keep you prepared to land uphill if suddenly necessary.

Field Surface

The surface of a field is not as important for ultralights as it is for regular aircraft but it should certainly be considered. A recently plowed or mulched field would probably mean a very quick stop and a difficult retrieve but usually not damaging, providing touchdown was into the wind at stall speed.

Pasture

Short grass and pasture is a good landing place, except for small hollows and bumps. Pasture land is not often tilled so it is lumpy. Domestic animals may stampede or, out of curiosity, come over and chew on the fabric if the plane is left alone.

Crops

Growing crops can be damaged by a landing or a taxiing ultralight, while tall crops are almost sure to cause damage to the plane. Corn or wheat has immense drag at 25 mph and can tear off the tail, hook a wing tip, or flip the whole plane upside down. If you must land in a long crop, such as corn, pretend the top is the surface and stall onto it so the plane will drop straight in and not slide through the crop very far.

Estimating the height of the crop from the air is extremely difficult — I know! I was out of lift but over what appeared to be a smooth field with short, green winter wheat. As my glider settled in for a landing, just ticking the tops, it seemed as if a giant hand grabbed the wing and threw me sideways! The glider dropped through the wheat, hit a small rut, and rolled over.

TOO HIGH TO ESTIMATE
ALTITUDE VERY ACCURATELY.

500 FT.

400 FT.

300 FT.

ERRORS ARE LESS WHEN YOU CAN
COMPARE YOUR HEIGHT WITH TREES,
BUILDINGS OR POLES.

200 FT.

100 FT.

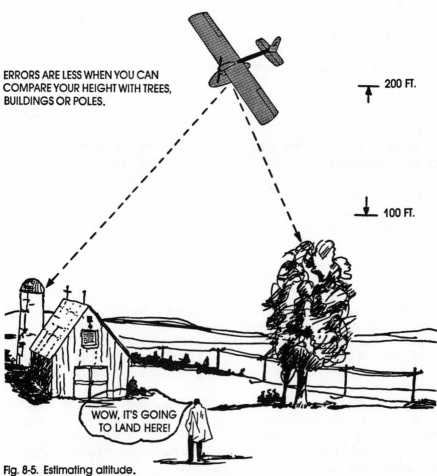

WOW, IT'S GOING
TO LAND HERE!

Fig. 8-5. Estimating altitude.

I thought someone had beat me over the head with a club, when I painfully crawled out of the wreckage. I found the wing torn off, rear spar snapped, the entire aft fuselage twisted off, and the cockpit split open all the way back to the wings, not to mention a smashed canopy and bent control tubes. The year of spare time spent repairing to get flying again made an impression — never land in tall crops! Check the height of growing plants as you drive out to the airport because it's almost impossible to guess from the air.

Picking Fields

While in cruise, look out at general areas such as smooth fields and open spaces. As you approach, begin choosing exact fields. When almost overhead, mentally set up a pattern and landing. Concentrate on obstructions such as: trees, wires, slope and surface of the field, and the possibility of livestock. Continue to check far ahead as you go on. This continual thinking about possibilities far ahead, medium and near, will keep you ready for the best forced landing.

If you are over unlandable country, pick the least of the worst. Perhaps a factory roof top will do. It might be a lot better than a shopping mall parking lot full of cars. Even in the middle of a big city there are often surprisingly many places to land — warehouse storage grounds, lakeshores and river banks, or empty playgrounds. Over rocky and mountainous country, look for rounded hilltops, the widest streambeds, tiny meadows and fire trails.

Estimating Altitude

Learning to guess your altitude away from home is important. The altimeter may be useless because the land over which you're flying is very often a different height than your home field. The last 400 feet are critical to final approach and landing. Practice estimating by blanking out the last 400 feet of your altimeter when flying around your home field. At 200 feet, trees and buildings can be used to give a direct comparison of your height to the ground. Very large fields or dry lakes have nothing with which to reference your height. In the dim light of dusk, one of my students couldn't sense her height above the surface of El Mirage Dry Lake. She thought the ground was farther away than it was, did not level out upon landing and smacked into the lake bed in a cloud of dust "and-a-Hi-Ho-Silver." No damage, but a good lesson. Even in perfect weather, estimating height above featureless ground is tricky. Look far ahead and edge down slowly, expecting the ground anytime. This should always be done in such places because you at least have the advantage of almost unlimited space.

Landing on Roads

In very rocky places or over forests, the only place to land may be a road. Watch for the slope, wires and fences, and traffic. Try to land uphill. Go under the wires if necessary because if you hook a wing you can be thrown sideways and flipped inverted in a flash. If the traffic is heavy, fit into a space between cars as close to the one ahead as you can, going with the flow. If it is not a divided highway but is a narrow two-way road, use special care.

For example, flying my little homebuilt glider from El Mirage to Las Vegas, I was about 140 miles out trying to follow the road up 7,000 foot Clark Mountain on the California-Nevada border. The thermals tired late in the afternoon and I was down to what looked to be 300 feet above the highway gamely riding each bit of lift whirled off by passing traffic. Suddenly, I saw a big truck blocking a line of cars behind. That was the chance I was looking for! I raced as far ahead as the plane could glide and touched on the centerline. I then edged to the side of the road and when very, very slow, drove into the ditch. There was much crackling and crunching of weeds as it went down the 12 foot embankment, but no damage and I was safely out of traffic's way.

Another time, several years later but at this same place and time believe it or not, I was back floating down the road at 300 feet. This time only one car was in sight. It was coming toward me at high speed. I elected to land down slope because of the strong west wind. "No problem, I thought, I'll just hold off until the car goes under me." As I flew 15 feet above the road, the car coming toward me, the unexpected happened to both of us. I swear I could see his eyes get like baseballs as he slammed on the brakes to stop ahead of me, exactly where I planned to touchdown! Thank goodness for the extra speed and slight downslope. I had just enough to pass over the car and land. He kindly helped me push the plane off the road, still wondering from what planet I had come.

If the Highway Patrol comes along, they will not let you take off and insist you disassemble the plane and transport it away. It's a good idea to pull the plane some distance off the road as soon as you can. You can always say you landed on the field next to the road in case the officer wants to make trouble. Perhaps "part" of your landing was on the road but you can neglect mentioning that. Several times I have landed on roads in the desert and had people go zooming right on past as if I had been a flying saucer. A few times, no one at all passed by.

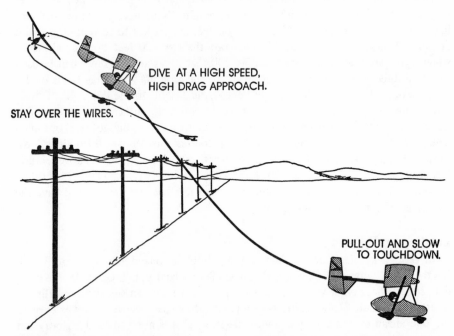

DIVE AT A HIGH SPEED, HIGH DRAG APPROACH.

STAY OVER THE WIRES.

PULL-OUT AND SLOW TO TOUCHDOWN.

IF THERE ARE HARD OBSTACLES AHEAD, PUT IT ON THE GROUND IMMEDIATELY TO REDUCE GROUNDSPEED. DRIVE ON THE GROUND TO DISSIPATE ENERGY.

Fig. 8-6. Clearing obstructions with the high energy approach to landing.

Clearing Obstructions

On approaches into a small field with trees or wires at the downwind end, stay close to the landing area. By gliding along one side and looking it over carefully, you can spot holes, tall weeds, irrigation pipes, ditches, or any details that might hurt the plane. This is called the downwind leg and should be flown at minimum sink speed.

When you reach the end of your landing place, where there is a line of wires, trees, or high ground, turn to fly along over the obstruction and begin adding speed for the "high-energy-approach." You can kill extra altitude over the obstruction by making a "beat" back and forth before turning in for the final leg. This is like an longated S-turn. **Never, ever, make a circle over the end of your landing place!** I know you may think you are very high, and a circle is the only way to get down close to the field however, this has brought more pilots to grief with forced landings than any other mistake. The downwind part of the circle will carry you much farther away from the field than you planned, and you can't see your landing spot since you're going away from it.

To keep position in the downwind part of the circle, as explained in the section in downwind turns, the bank must be very steep which increases the stalling speed. The possibility of stalling or spinning by nervously misusing the controls, is very great. When the plane does come around into the wind, you may find it is much stronger than you estimated when you were higher. There may not be enough height to pass over the obstruction. A circling approach, after lots of practice at the home field, can be done, but why make things difficult? A series of S-turns over the obstructions at the end of the landing spot are just as effective in using up extra height, and you are always in a position to make a turn and put it in the field whenever you feel you are low enough. By practicing sharp, steep turns, you can be confident in bringing the plane down very steeply over obstructions.

Low obstructions such as ditches, fences, and rocks should be flown over with extra speed so you can have some energy to use in pulling up to extend the glide. Once you are over the obstructions and close to the ground, slow the plane to let it stall from a foot. In case you misread the surface, any ditches or rocks hidden in the field are struck with much less force.

One exception to the rule of minimum speed touchdown is when there is a big tree, wall, pile of rocks or buildings ahead of you with no way to avoid striking. Put the ultralight on the ground as soon as you can, even if the surface is rough or brushy and your speed high. Dissipating energy on the ground is uncomfortable but better than smacking into an immovable object even at stall speed.

Forced Versus Planned or Precautionary Landings

A forced landing is different than a planned landing because you must immediately do the best job possible within gliding range. All decisions must be made in relation to "least bad," and executed immediately. Some landings are more leisurely. You may want to stop to refuel and check the engine, relieve yourself, eat, do some map planning or stop for the night.

Fly around, find the smoothest hill or flat field. At 300 feet you can circle a prospective field for as long as you wish, or even make simulated non-touch and goes. It is particularly easy to adjust the final approach with the throttle so you can drive up to the edge of the field and cut it to make a perfect spot

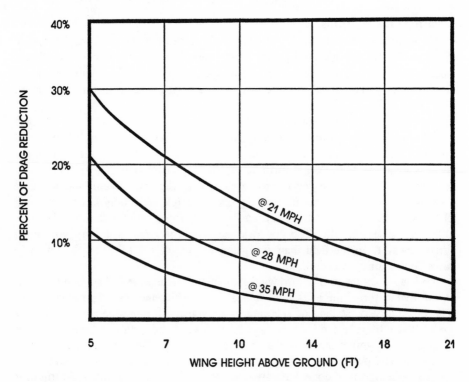

WING HEIGHT ABOVE GROUND (FT)

IF THE AIRCRAFT IS NOT STALLED, THERE IS NEVER ANY REASON FOR IT TO FALL WHEN FLOWN OUT OF GROUND EFFECT, BECAUSE IT WILL SETTLE BACK TOWARD THE GROUND AND THE LOW DRAG AREA, AND CONTINUE FLYING. GROUND EFFECT IS OFTEN BLAMED FOR ACCIDENTS THAT ARE ACTUALLY THE RESULT OF CLIMBING TOO STEEPLY AND STALLING OUT.

IF THE PILOT PULLS-UP TOO QUICKLY, THE AIRCRAFT MAY NOT HAVE ENOUGH POWER TO OVERCOME THE INCREASED DRAG.

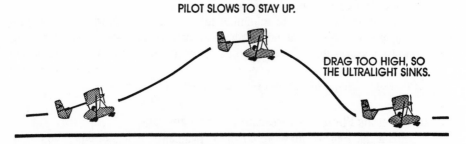

AS THE ULTRALIGHT NEARS THE GROUND, IT SETTLES INTO THE GROUND EFFECT.
AT THE SLOW, ALMOST STALLED AIRSPEED OF 21 MPH, THE DRAG IS REDUCED 40%, ALLOWING THE AIRCRAFT TO CONTINUE FLYING EASILY.

Fig. 8-7. How drag reduces in ground effect.

Another kind of planned landing is when you wish to stop at a specific place, such as in the field behind your friend's house or near a food or fuel station. This kind of landing may be very difficult. Repeat your pattern several times, checking the wind, being extra careful to curve around or drop over obstructions. When it's time to land, use the same techniques as in a forced landing, except come in over obstructions a little bit slower because you can always add power if you've misjudged. Once clear, dive to the ground, level off, lose speed and touch at the stall.

Always think of your takeoff when picking fields. You may have a clear approach into a smooth, little field but have 75 foot trees at the upwind end making a climb out difficult in "dead air."

Rough Field Takeoff

A rough field takeoff, with or without wind, should be made slowly for least wear and tear on the ultralight. As soon as the plane has picked up enough speed for control effectiveness, the nose should be pitched to best climb position for a quick, slow takeoff. If the field is soft or rough, it's better to get the plane in the air to stop the pounding on the landing gear and other parts. After the plane is off, it may make a few gentle bounces or skips, but that does little harm. When the plane is flying, the speed should be increased, being very careful not to nose down too much and strike the ground. It's best to hold the plane almost at the stall until you're about three feet high. Then, nose down to pick up speed to either best rate of climb or best angle of climb, depending on obstruction. Remember, best angle of climb will get you up, out of a more confined space.

Trespassing

You may have done a dozen landings in various fields and had nothing but friendly welcomes. Sooner or later though, you'll run into an angry, suspicious person who talks of "crop damage," trespassing, calling the deputies or the F.A.A. This person may demand payment for real or imagined damages, or whatever. Since you have had good relations in the past, and you know nothing was damaged you may get angry with this character and become defensive in return, but don't do it. The law is on the ground person's side.

By accepting the landowner's position of authority, you can defuse what could be an escalating situation. Country people often have a possessive, almost paranoid, view of land that we, who are accustomed to cities, do not understand. Most city land is shared and neighbors are very close. We think nothing of neighbor kids picking up a ball that's bounced into our yard, or recognizing others' rights to be in the park. Not so with many isolated people.

Once I landed my Flying Wing glider and clipped an irrigation pipe fitting, slightly cracking it. I jumped the fence to telephone my crew from a nearby gas station with directions to find me, then went back to the glider. The parachute, worth $600, was gone!

I walked to the house where the farmer sat on his porch with a gun, for "crissakes," and my parachute on his lap. He was being a jerk, but I knew my crew was coming in a few minutes and wanted to get out of there. I agreed immediately to pay him for the cracked fitting, completely sympathized with his position and contritely thanked him for having such a wonderful place to save me. I told him I was in his debt forever for being able to land on his property. No matter how unfair and arbitrary, he was demanding an exhorbitant amount for the fitting, besides keeping my parachute. I realized, after all, that it was his land I was using. I accepted the landowners position of authority by agreeing with him. "You can keep my parachute until you're satisfied that I have completely made good whatever damage I have caused." His attitude softened. Once he saw that I was understanding, I was able to turn on more charm and discuss flying adventures, farming, and explain about unexpected landings. By the time the crew arrived we were having drinks on the porch, the gun was put away and he said to forget about the fitting.

An efficious person may not even be a landowner. No matter. What anyone really wants is acceptance of their authority, and understanding. So, go along with them. Understanding is seldom accomplished between antagonists when one points out the stupidity and unfairness of the other.

Mental Practice

You can enhance your skills greatly while you're driving in your car to the ultralight airport. Assess the fields you pass for possible landings. Look for signs of the wind, check for power lines and other obstructions, note slopes and surface textures. You can see how this same field looks from the air. As you ride past, quickly think, "Let's see now. If I came in over those wires, then went between the trees, I could aim for that little bare spot and be stopped before the ditch here at the end. Or maybe, if I came in the other way, kiddy corner, I would have more room to get stopped in the smooth spot, because I can come in lower." Look at hills and picture landing uphill near the top. If you're driving through hilly country, look down at lower hills to check the surface for rocks and holes. Later, see how the same hills and fields appear from the air and perhaps practice some patterns around these landing places. Can you really see the steepness of that slope from the air that is so easy to spot from the ground? Do this when you're driving and always consider approaches from various directions. You will be well repaid in the ability to make the kind of quick decisions based on a lot of inputs so necessary for forced landings and off-field operations.

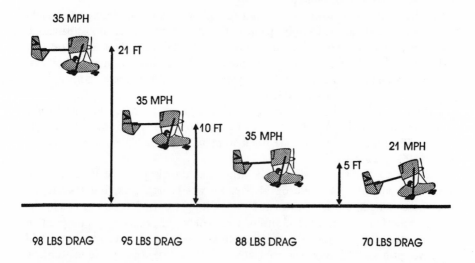

Fig. 8-8. Illustrating drag reduction in proximity to the ground. Assume the ultralight has an even 100 pounds of drag in level flight, at altitude. At slow speeds near the ground, the induced drag is reduced proportionately more than at high speed at altitude.

Ground Effect

When a plane takes off and is barely into the air, it may fail to climb and fall heavily back to earth. It has been thought this was caused by flying out of the ground effect. Ground effect occurs within half a wingspan of the ground because the drag due to lift is reduced. The downwash of the wing hits the ground and flattens out. For the same amount of lift the wing, therefore, does not have to deflect the air as much. This "cushion" of air near the ground may help the plane get into the air, but once out of the effect the plane will drop. It sounds very theoretical, but like the wind gradient in downwind turns, it's not the total answer. Ninety percent of the phenomena supposedly due to ground effect are mistaken observations. What really happens in the "ground effect" accident is that the pilot begins climbing before his speed has built up. When the speed slows during the climb, the plane will come down. If the angle of attack is less than stalling and the speed is above stall, the plane will not drop, no matter if it is flying out of the ground effect or not. On landing, the pilot floats over the ground because his speed is gradually bleeding off, not because the plane is gliding along in ground effect.

AIR THINS WITH ALTITUDE AS WELL AS TEMPERATURE.

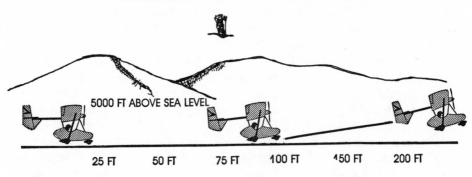

5000 FT ABOVE SEA LEVEL

25 FT   50 FT   75 FT   100 FT   150 FT   200 FT

THE ENGINE LOSES ABOUT TWO PERCENT OF ITS POWER FOR EACH THOUSAND FEET ABOVE SEA LEVEL. THE WINGS NEED TWO PERCENT MORE TRUE AIRSPEED PER THOUSAND FEET TO LIFT (THE AIRSPEED HOWEVER, READS THE SAME). THE AIRCRAFT HAS REACHED ITS CEILING WHEN IT CAN NO LONGER CLIMB.

SEA LEVEL TAKEOFF

25 FT   50 FT   75 FT   100 FT   150 FT   200 FT

Fig. 8-9. Altitude and temperature increases decrease performance.

Heat and Altitude Effect

Although ground effect is a misunderstood phenomenon, in takeoff accidents where the plane falls back to the ground, heat and altitude effects are very real. For each 1,000 feet above sea level, the air loses two percent of its density and, therefore, the engine can not produce as much power. As we saw in the chapter on thermals, heat will also make the air thinner. Taking off from a hot, high altitude runway can double or triple the run. Once, I flew a Volkswagon powered motorglider from an airport over 13,000 feet above sea level, on a cool day. This airplane usually took off after only a run of 500 feet. It used 3,200 feet to become airborne at that altitude!

Another time, during a takeoff from an Arizona runway at mid-day in 115 degree heat, the motorglider took 2,500 feet, even though elevation was only a couple thousand feet above sea level! Draw up a special chart for your ultralight by using the well-known Koch diagram, which can be found in the book, Ultralight Aircraft — The Basic Handbook of Ultralight Aviation.

Takeoffs from strange fields can be more difficult than landing because sensing when the ultralight isn't going to make it and stopping the attempt, is a decision filled with unknowns. An ultralight will get off the ground rather quickly, but climbing out with turbulence from trees ahead or surrounding hills may pull it down alarmingly. Should you keep going or shut down and put it back on the ground? Often, just when you think it's hopeless, the plane comes out of the wind gradient and leaps up easily out of danger.

In Japan, during the 1981 FAI World Hang Glider Championships, Joe Greblo, Chris Hartinian, and I were involved in an ultralight demonstration program. We were using the edge of Lake Shidaka for our 600 foot runway. There were lots of rollers and downs because we were surrounded by hills covered thickly with trees. We had a special Trike and a Pterodactyl with powerful Yamaha engines. Either would takeoff in from 4 to 6 seconds and climb out strongly. The pilot had to turn quickly to stay over the lake in order to miss the hills and trees. There seemed to be a downdraft just when the turn was required, as long as the wind was blowing.

Very early one sunny, calm appearing morning, Joe Greblo took off in the Trike and hit down at the usual place. It was so early and calm, the downdraft was unexpected. Joe thought there must be something wrong and cut the power for a straight-ahead landing on the smooth ground at the end of the lake. The trike pitched over when the nose wheel dug in. The "smooth ground" was soft mud! Not much damage, but what a splattered mess. We washed off the mud and resumed flying later that day. Joe thought, if he had simply kept going to the other side of the down it would probably have flown out safely. That is always the problem with takeoffs. You never know whether to keep it going another few seconds.

On takeoff from El Mirage Dry Lake in my motorglider, I had to run along the edge because the middle was full of water after a rainstorm. The surface was muddy and sticky which impeded my little 28 hp VW Fournier. It was accelerating, however, and soon the tail was up and the wings level, aileron balancing on the single wheel. I felt everything was fine and we could be in the air any instant. It was still "almost ready to takeoff" when the wheel hit some bumps and ripped off. The plane skidded to a stop with a smashed wing leading edge and a shattered propeller. Yet, there was no particular instant in which I felt that takeoff should have been stopped. That's why I say "takeoff accidents are most difficult to prevent

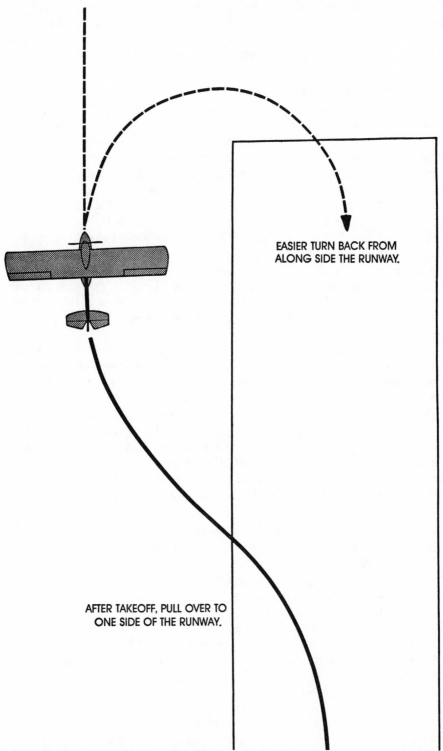

EASIER TURN BACK FROM
ALONG SIDE THE RUNWAY.

AFTER TAKEOFF, PULL OVER TO
ONE SIDE OF THE RUNWAY.

Fig. 8-10. Always pull off to one side of the runway on takeoff. This keeps other planes from running over you, and is safer in case of engine failure.

because of not knowing exactly when to stop." If there is several thousand feet available for takeoff with clear approaches all around, there is no doubt. In this case, if the plane isn't going to fly, it won't be because of external reasons. You can be pretty sure the engine or aircraft is at fault and abort the takeoff.

Engine Stops After Takeoff

If the engine quits after takeoff, the decision of stopping the flight has been done for you! Now the problem is whether or not to turn back. If the wind is blowing 10 to 12 mph or better, go straight ahead and land, even onto a poor surface, because your landing speed will be very low. Turning around would mean a downwind landing at over 30 mph, with a possible spin-out or ground loop at the end when you run out of wind pressure on the control surfaces.

If you're high enough to make a short pattern around and back into the wind for a landing, that's great. It's those in-between situations that require quick decisions and superb flying. The general rule is to go straight ahead because the landing speed should be low enough to cause only minor damage to the plane or minimal injury to the pilot. A stall, spin, or spiral dive out of an inept turn could on the other hand, be fatal. A superb pilot can do precision minimum altitude turns quickly, safely, and is thus able to make a wider range of decisions in the event of engine failure on takeoff. Again, watch the airspeed and yaw string and ignore the ground motion.

If the engine stops, nose down immediately in order to pick-up speed lost during the end of the climb, while the engine was losing power. Move the nose down smoothly. One pilot had his engine stopped because he was low on fuel. He jammed the nose down so quickly that some fuel was thrown up and reached the engine, which suddenly came to life at full power. The pilot did not have time to slow his speed by pulling up, and he was apparently unable to quickly throttle back. The ensuing power dive collapsed the overspeeded ultralight in mid-air. Lesson: If the engine fails on takeoff, shut it off. Concentrate on going to the proper airspeed and the landing, whether straight ahead or turning back. Do not fiddle with the engine and be distracted while the airspeed bleeds away.

Summary of Cross-Country in an Ultralight

- Practice traffic patterns in calm and wind, engine on and off.
- Use a small, tight pattern for airports.
- Line up with the runway center, only at the last second.
- Always know the wind direction as you fly.
- Land uphill, and take off downhill.
- Use cut, not growing crops for landing.
- Always watch for possible landing fields when flying or driving.
- If landing on a road, stay behind traffic and move quickly to the field alongside after touchdown.
- Never turn away from your field.
- S-turn to lose height over obstructions.
- It takes two to argue. Be friendly on others' property.
- Keep your eyes on the airspeed and slip indicators when turning back.

Chapter Nine~ Simplified Navigation for Ultralights

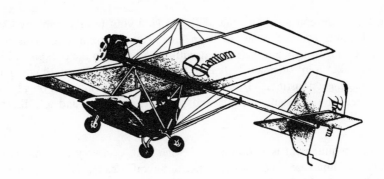

Simplified Navigation for Ultralights

When you are confident of your ability to land your ultralight in any kind of field and wind, you are ready to learn cross country navigation. This mainly concerns reading a map and matching it with the view from the cockpit. It sounds simple but takes a lot of practice. It is very easy to become lost until you develop the "homing-pigeon-instinct." It is much different than driving a car on a long trip because there are no signs, arrows, and places to pull over and ask directions.

Maps

The first requirement is a good map — either that, or a very good memory. At an airport training base, pilot supply store, or aircraft dealer, Sectional Charts can be had for a few dollars. (Do not get WAC Charts. World Aeronautical Charts cover too much area so the details are too small.) Along the bottom of these charts is a scale of miles, knots, and kilometers. There is much other valuable information about restricted areas and an excellent legend. Become familiar with the different markings and their meanings.

You can buy a plotter to use with the chart, or make your own by marking off a strip of paper from the scale at the bottom. Be sure to use the same scale units as you're own airspeed. Mark your takeoff spot and your planned goal. Then, draw a line between them, with each five miles marked along your line. Knowing how long the engine should run with the fuel you carry and an honest cruising speed,

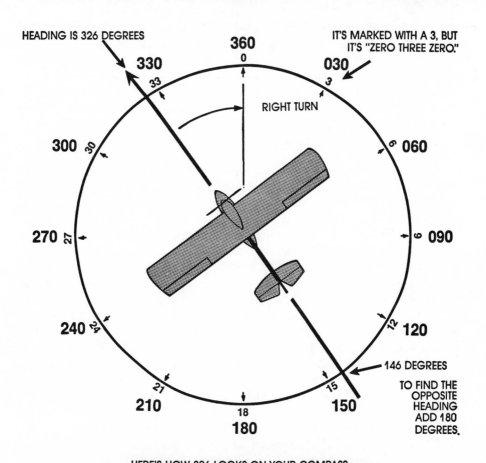

HEADING IS 326 DEGREES

IT'S MARKED WITH A 3, BUT IT'S "ZERO THREE ZERO."

RIGHT TURN

146 DEGREES

TO FIND THE OPPOSITE HEADING ADD 180 DEGREES.

HERE'S HOW 326 LOOKS ON YOUR COMPASS.

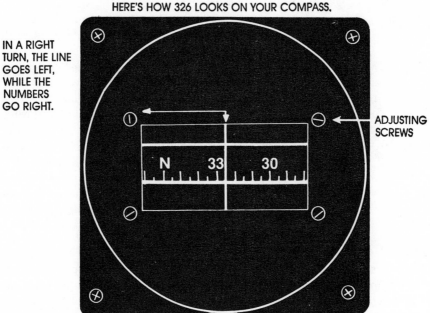

IN A RIGHT TURN, THE LINE GOES LEFT, WHILE THE NUMBERS GO RIGHT.

ADJUSTING SCREWS

Fig. 9-1. Using the compass to navigate.

will show if you can make your destination with enough reserve in case you have headwinds, get lost or the engine uses more fuel than expected. At the speed you fly, say a mile every two minutes, you can mark the flying time for the entire trip, starting with zero at takeoff. Try to find unmistakable checkpoints such as: power lines, major highways and intersections, mountains, rivers, railroads, or radio towers. Many of these can be seen on your airplane Sectional Chart. Circle them and mark the time you anticipate being there after takeoff.

Compass

I have found a standard aircraft compass the best for navigation. They can be had inexpensively as used at many airplane supply stores and airports. Car and boat compasses could be used in desperation, but the boat types are difficult to mount and the car units seem imprecise. On your Sectional Chart there is a Compass Rose around many of the VOR stations. The heading numbers around the stations are already compensated for the magnetic deviation of your area so you can use them directly. Using a parallelogram ruler or simply sliding a single ruler, draw a line through the compass, parallel to your course. Your compass heading will be the number found under the line and on the outside edge of the VOR Compass Rose in the direction you plan to go. Write that number along your course line with an arrow pointing in the direction you're going. Draw another arrow pointing toward your home field. It's the compass heading for finding your way back.

Most airports have a Compass Rose painted on a taxiway. Mount your compass on the ultralight, take it to the Compass Rose at a nearby airport and "swing" your plane to each heading to see what your compass says in relation to the one on the ground. If you cannot use the adjustments to make them coincide, mount a small card near the face of your compass showing the correct headings.

A good auto map published by one of the insurance clubs, AAA etc., is good for beginning navigation because you're more at home with it. Again, draw your lines, mark the distance and times, the most noted landmarks, and transfer any obstructions from the airplane map to the car map with the heights noted. With two maps you can more easily corrulate with what's on the ground.

Next drive your planned course in a car. Watch for and note landing fields on both maps and try to picture how they will look from the air. For your first trips, stay away from trackless swamps and mountains. From the air things look very different. You will see roads and curves you may have never noticed while driving. A steep hill flattens out when seen from the air. A perfect landing field you may have noted from the ground may be impossible to find from 1,000 feet. Two small towns may be very different seen from your car, but may be unbelievably identical from the air.

In a car we are often not as aware of direction as we are in the air. Practice estimating directions as you drive. Notice where the sun is during various times of the day. It could save you from getting lost.

Restricted Areas

The basics presented here are only enough to get around and keep from getting too lost or interfering with other airplanes. There are so many individual cases and details, depending on where you wish to fly, they could fill another book explaining all the "ifs," "ands," and "buts." The easiest and very best way to learn more is to take your map to a pilot or flight instructor and have that person show you if

1) IN AN AIRPORT TRAFFIC AREA. THIS IS FIVE MILES AROUND AN AIRFIELD WITH AN OPERATING CONTROL TOWER, FROM GROUND TO 3000 FEET ABOVE GROUND LEVEL (AGL).

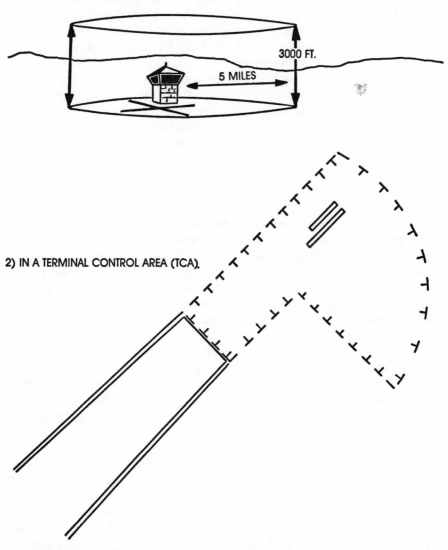

2) IN A TERMINAL CONTROL AREA (TCA).

3) A RESTRICTED OR PROHIBITED AREA .... DON'T BUZZ MILITARY BASES OR THE WHITE HOUSE!

Fig. 9-2. The primary three areas you may not fly over without a clearance from the controlling authorities.

there are any restricted areas, what the restrictions are, pointing out where air traffic is likely and how to pass near other airports or suggest alternatives. Briefly, you can fly almost anywhere below 1,200 feet above the ground if you can see one mile, and up to 3,000 feet if the visibility is three miles. Out in the, boonies there are many restricted areas usually reserved for military operations. Read about each one. You can often fly under the MOA (Military Operations Area) with an ultralight and some are opened on weekends.

Strap the maps to your legs with a pen, and attach a pencil so it won't blow away. At takeoff, set your watch to the nearest even hour or use the stop watch part of your "Casio." You should stop timing when you want to circle something of interest, gain altitude, or pause for any reason. Restart your watch when again on course. This way you will know when your check points should arrive. After a good deal of experience in a particular airplane, you'll develop a sense of time and distance almost naturally just as in a car.

Crosswinds

The direction you fly, according to what you wrote on your course line and the actual way you must point the plane to get where you're going, is often different because there is a crosswind. The wind is not blowing on the plane or blowing the plane around. The air mass in which the plane is suspended is simply moving at an angle to your course over the ground. To compensate, you must "crab" over the ground. Remember, a crab is not a skid, or a slip, or a turn. The crab angle is the difference between your track over the ground and your heading.

To compensate for a crosswind when you don't know its speed or direction, requires seeing a checkpoint ahead of you on the course. If you take off and begin heading toward that big chimney, building or tower, or perhaps flying along a highway, you may find that the plane keeps drifting to one side or another. You can keep aiming at the checkpoint until you arrive, but the plane will describe a large curved path over the ground, requiring you to change your heading up to as much as 90 degrees. This works fine if you have easily seen checkpoints and you fly from one to the next, but it's inefficient and imprecise.

A better way is to aim to one side of the checkpoint, compensating for the movement of the air mass. For example, you find that a compass heading of 240 degrees (24 on the window), keeps moving you to the right of the checkpoint. Turn to a heading of 21, for example, and keep flying in that direction. You may notice your checkpoint is now to your right, yet the plane moves directly toward it. Moving sideways, relative to the ground, is called "crabbing." You'll also notice that smoke, flags, or cloud shadows will show a wind from the left. Your heading of 210 means there is a 30 degree compensation for the wind. This heading should be flown as long as the wind doesn't change. If the next checkpoint is so far away it can't be seen clearly, or perhaps haze is limiting visibility, keep going on the heading you were and wait for it to come in view at the proper time.

The ideal situation is when you can see two checkpoints at the same time. By using them like a gun site, you can set a very precise heading. For night navigation during World War One, two search lights were set on course with their beams pointing straight up. The pilots would take off in their bombers and use the searchlight beams for checkpoints to get to and from the target at night.

A wind directly on the nose or tail will require no heading compensation but the time between checkpoints will vary. If you keep arriving too soon, there is a

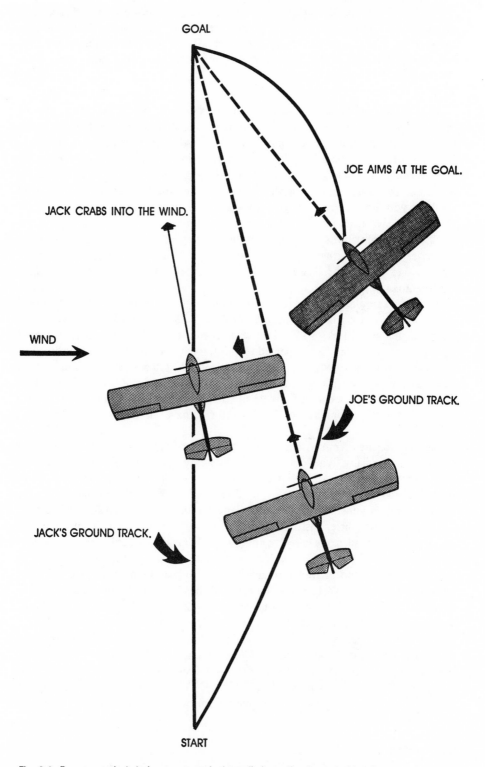

GOAL

JOE AIMS AT THE GOAL.

JACK CRABS INTO THE WIND.

WIND

JOE'S GROUND TRACK.

JACK'S GROUND TRACK.

START

Fig. 9-3. Proper control during a crosswind results in a direct ground track.

135

tailwind, or perhaps the airspeed is wrong and your plane cruises faster than estimated. In a headwind, or if the airspeed reads too fast, checkpoints would take longer. The most common reasons for checkpoints coming up at the wrong time are: misreading the time or measuring incorrectly on the map. Double check your calculations.

Lost

Pilots never get lost! They're going along very well and everything is coming along in sight as planned. There's that river ahead, next comes the lake, then another river, and the flyer is complacent. Then a river appears that isn't anywhere it should be...or maybe a big town. You weren't lost, but all of a sudden someone moved things around when you weren't looking and nothing is matching up anymore. The usual reason for this is not marking the time as you go along and thinking you are farther than you really are. The river you thought was a check-point may have been only a tributary. We all tend to be optimists and we often mark a checkpoint too soon and enjoy the good speed we're making. The truth is, we're very seldom farther than we thought we should be. Keeping track of your time is one of the surest ways to keep from being fooled by similar looking checkpoints.

A good example was my experience during a glider contest in which we had a 250 mile speed task from El Mirage to Amboy, California and back, Every second counts in the speed tasks, so I had marked my map carefully and estimated where I should be at each hour, if I expected to win the day. I climbed in the whirling dust devils as tightly and slowly as possible, catching each stall with a quick pump of the stick, and when the lift weakened, sped on. "There's Lavic Dry Lake" below. Great! I'm making good time." I headed straight across the lake. In another hour I could see the turning point ahead. "I'm going to have the fastest speed for sure," I thought.

As I approached Amboy, I noticed it didn't look right. Another ten miles and I had the shock of my flying career. I was coming up to Twenty-nine Palms, which is over 30 miles south of Amboy! I was so embarassed and angry with myself, I was ready to bail out. I had made the typical error of thinking I was farther than I was by mistaking an unnamed, insignificant dry lake for Lavic. This little lake had been just north of my course. I assumed there was a south wind and my "compensation" quite properly headed me directly for Twenty-nine Palms. Unbelieveably, I won after all because I hit the Granddaddy of all dust devils over the rocky ridge going north to Amboy and arrived thousands of feet higher than the rest of the competitors. I was thus able to make the turn and head back to El Mirage quickly. My friends said lift was scant over the center of the course so they all had gone far to the north to find lift, and had gone about as far out of the way as I did!

This is the typical story of being lost, and the lesson is to mark your time and make sure you're at the checkpoint. When planning, think of all the ways you can mistake checkpoints. Make notations on each site of places you might notice, if you drift off course. This is called "bracketing." You could use a highway on one side or a river on the other, so you have some idea to which side of the course you're off.

Triangulation

Big landmarks can help you find an unknown position by drawing a line in the direction you are heading. Then, take a guess at the angle of certain landmarks you can see on the ground, as well as on your map. Draw a light line from the landmark to your heading line. Now turn and take a sighting to a landmark on the other side. Where your lines cross will be close to your present position.

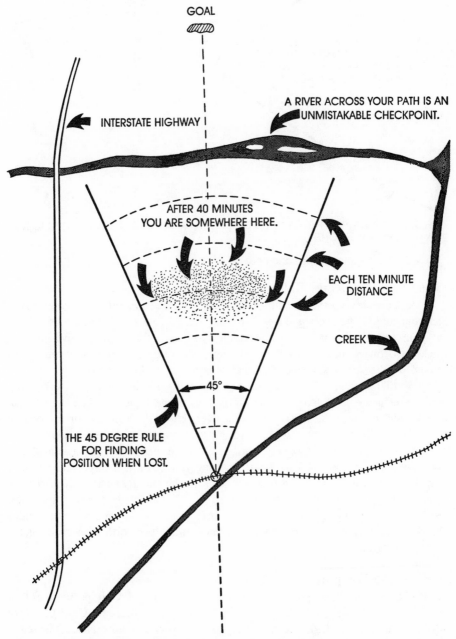

GOAL

A RIVER ACROSS YOUR PATH IS AN UNMISTAKABLE CHECKPOINT.

INTERSTATE HIGHWAY

AFTER 40 MINUTES YOU ARE SOMEWHERE HERE.

EACH TEN MINUTE DISTANCE

CREEK

45°

THE 45 DEGREE RULE FOR FINDING POSITION WHEN LOST.

Fig. 9-4. By marking your map with known boundary checkpoints ahead of time, you can always spot your general position.

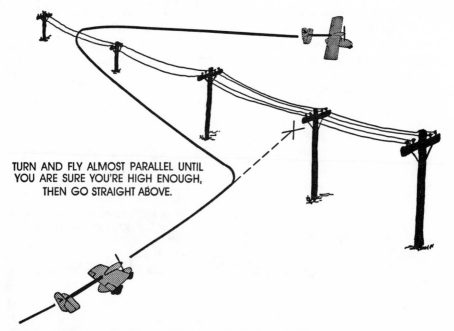

TURN AND FLY ALMOST PARALLEL UNTIL
YOU ARE SURE YOU'RE HIGH ENOUGH,
THEN GO STRAIGHT ABOVE.

NEVER GO STRAIGHT OVER BECAUSE IT'S DIFFICULT TO JUDGE HEIGHT AND DIFFICULT TO TURN AWAY AT THE LAST SECOND.

Fig. 9-5. Crossing power lines and trees

The Forty-five Degree Rule

Practice using your thumb and forefinger in making ten minute distance estimates on your map. If you miss a checkpoint and don't know where you are, look back at your last checkpoint. If, for example, you have flown twenty-five minutes, make two finger measures plus a little more, then swing an imaginary one-eighth circle. You're surely someplace in that area and probably on the outer edge. If there is still no recognizable place, keep your compass heading and again, using your fingers, estimate how long you must fly until some important line across your course will be reached. This could be a river, interstate highway, or railroad. It should cover at least 45 degrees in front of you. If you suspect there is a crosswind, do not try to counter it by guess work, but instead, maintain your heading. When you do arrive at the major landmark crossing your path, it is important to know which way to turn in order to follow it back to the line. By letting any drift carry you one way, you will know which way to turn. For example, if you're flying east with wind from the north, and you suspect your checkpoints are not coming because you may be south of the course line, simply turn north when reaching the cross landmark.

Believe The Compass

If there are no checkpoints and you're truly unsure of your position, follow that compass heading faithfully. In 1980 I was flying over the Gran Chaco of Bolivia and Paraguay trying to head toward Ascension in a motorglider. The sea of jungle had no aiming points anywhere! I would be puttering along looking down at the jungle, wondering if there really was a tribe of beautiful Amazons that needed a

138

male to service them. When I broke from my reverie, I noticed the compass was misreading 30 degrees. I was sure the plane was going in the correct direction, same as before, and the compass was wrong. I turned back to the 120 heading, almost reluctantly, and kept going. Several hours later the Mennonite Settlement of Filidelphia appeared, the only checkpoint in that sea of trees. Of course, the compass was right.

Summary of Simplified Navigation for Ultralights
- Mark your maps with time, distance and checkpoints.
- Learn to read, use and trust the compass.
- Have an instructor explain your Sectional Chart.
- Compensate for a crosswind by heading into it.
- Know your "time-in-flight" estimate locations.
- Cross check your position, use your heading and the direction to two distant landmarks.
- Insure finding your way by using major features crossing your path and on each side of the course, along with knowing your time from the last position.

Chapter Ten~
Keep an
Ultra-low Profile

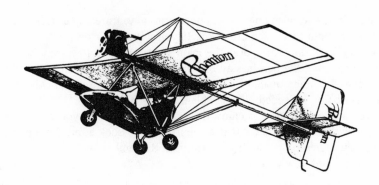

Keep an Ultra·low Profile

Have all the challenging experiences and adventures you can, flying your ultralight without attracting attention. If you wish to fly over a town, go straight over–going back and forth over the main street or down low, may bring trouble. When flying along the beach, stay out over the water and go right on past. If you have a forced landing or make a precautionary stop, move on quickly and quietly with a takeoff or, if needed, disassemble the aircraft.

If you are really flying to enjoy the experience yourself, you can do just about anything with no problems, but if the purpose is, "Look at me, hero pilot," there is a greatly increased possibility of trouble. Remember the old saying, "It's not what you do, but how you do it."

There are times when any flyer could be in violation of FAA rules. There are also always a certain percentage of people who don't want others to have fun. They seem to believe life should be full of "purpose" and hard work and rules should govern. These types are attracted to legislative and bureaucratic positions where their philosophies often have a good deal of influence. Their thinking is, "Yes, you can have fun provided you don't smile when you're doing it." This seems to be the basis for many regulations involving flying.

For example, pilots are required to have a medical certificate to fly a powered airplane. This medical certificate must be renewed every two years, in the case of a private pilot. It sounds like a good idea except there is not one iota of evidence to show the (slight) safety value, to flying, of this ritual that costs pilots and tax-payers an estimated $40,000,000 a year.

The Federal Aviation Administration authorities say, "Ultralights and experimental airplanes are not to fly over populated or congested areas." Why this rather vague rule exists is unclear. Uncertificated aircraft, such as homebuilts, have accident rates, due to mechanical failures, identical to regular factory-made airplanes. Yet, there have been many people killed and injured by commercial aircraft falling on them, or engines and parts dropping off, as they flew over the cities. An ultralight would do little more than bend a TV antenna if it crashed into a city! If you suspect many rules were thought up to keep people from "having fun," you would be correct. Any of us can think of very logical reasons to make prohibitions about anything a human being does. Guard your freedoms. Don't give those who think regulation is the answer to everything, a chance to limit flying. How? Keep a low profile, an "ultra-low" profile.

What would you do if you got a call, "This is Officer Doright of the Highway Patrol. I got a report that you were going 67 mph on the Interstate last Tuesday. What's your story about it? You would probably explain you didn't know what he was talking about and be quite insulted to be asked a self-incriminating question in violation of your Constitutional Fifth Amendment Rights.

Pilots generally do the opposite when the FAA calls to ask for an explanation of a possible FAR violation. Perhaps it's the image of uniqueness, being a "hero flyer," or happiness at getting attention. Who knows? Invariably, pilots will incriminate themselves with explanations.

As a court approved expert witness in an ultralight case, I have discussed this with lawyers and legal experts. It is appropriate to tell you their advice. They say it is most difficult to defend pilots because the flyer has already made the case for the FAA.

Legally, it is much more difficult to convict a flyer than a driver. For example, a pilot must be positively identified as the flyer of the plane during the alleged incident. This is almost impossible to prove, without the pilot admitting it. Height above the ground, distance from people, again, is open to doubt on cross examination by a defense lawyer. The FAA cannot legally assess a fine! You can only be fined after conviction in a court of law. As it is now, with the FAA assessing penalties, it is as if the police themselves could fine a person for a traffic violation. The FAA fines "informally" and will probably continue to do so until some wealthy and/or highly motivated person makes a case of their present procedures.

Here's how it works. An FAA official will call. "You were seen flying low over a group of people out at the park, doing turns and dives. What's your story?" You may explain that your friends asked you to fly over the office picnic and you really weren't lower than 150 feet. You also say you went at least two miles away from the local airport in going to and from the park, etc., etc. The FAA person will encourage you to explain why and what you were doing, and may seem to agree with your belief that your actions were perfectly safe under the circumstances. The conversation may end with you feeling very contrite and apologetic, with the FAA person implying that everything is okay, "now that you have explained."

A few days later, the FAA official calls back explaining that, "his boss insists something be done about it" and you may be asked to pay a $200 fine.

Lawyers advise to keep quiet because most pilots "explanations" contain the seeds of other violations beside the one that brought on the attention of the FAA. They say, if asked, do not make any statement. You don't have to. You may ask them exactly who said you were flying where they say you were flying, and with what you are being charged. If the FAA is not willing to furnish this precise information, there is no reason for you to fill it in for them. Lawyers insist you do not answer any leading questions no matter how friendly and seemingly helpful and informal the official may be. These lawyers do not condone dangerous flying or bothering people on the ground, but the nature of aviation is such that people can often misunderstand what a flyer is doing. Slope soaring, even on an isolated ridge, can seem like "buzzing" to people hiking on the mountain.

Happy flying is safe flying, and safe flying is knowing all the things that might go wrong, while having the ability and confidence to handle them properly. I hope some of the ideas of airmanship presented here will be a beginning in your advance toward being a superbly experienced and skilled ultralight pilot. I hope you will become a "master of the air."

Summary of Keep an Ultra-low Profile

- Fly unnoticed to keep "their-oughta-be-a-law" people from proscribing your freedom.
- Silence is golden.
- Flying is a very personal achievement – don't make a spectacle of yourself.
- Always think "Safety."

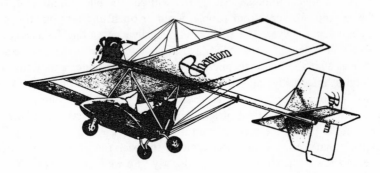